To Sha

With best wishes,
Darin

YOU CAN COME HOME AGAIN

Musings and Amusings of a
Philosopher-Clergyman

Davin Wolok, Ph.D.

Printed in the United States of America
Published by WingSpan Press, Livermore, CA
www.wingspanpress.com
The WingSpan name, logo and colophon are the trademarks of WingSpan Publishing.

First Edition 2010
ISBN 978-1-59594-377-4
Library of Congress Control Number: 2010923027

To my wife Carol

"An indomitable spirit who can find?
Her value exceeds every measure."

—Proverbs 31:10

'Where is the dwelling of God?'

This is the question with which the Rabbi of Kotzk surprised a number of learned men who happened to be visiting him.

They laughed at him: 'What a thing to ask! Is not the whole world full of his glory?'

Then he answered his own question.

'God dwells wherever man lets him in.'

Martin Buber, *The Way of Man: According to the Teaching of Hasidism*

TABLE OF CONTENTS

INTRODUCTION

Two experiences, one spanning eighty years.

A baby is comfortably sitting on his mother's lap in an office of the immigration service of the United States. It is 1920, and the family of three has just arrived from Poland. Like most other Jews from the "old country," the mother barely knows English, and she struggles to comprehend the question which is being posed to her. The agent asks her, "What is your son's name?" She doesn't understand. Then he asks again, "What is your son's name?" This time he somehow connects, and she answers, "Yerachmiel," which means "God shall be merciful." The agent says, "What?" And she repeats, "Yerachmiel." He writes down, "Emil," which has been my father's name ever since.

In a different setting, decades later, I am approached by the mother of a boy who will become Bar Mitzvah in the year 2000. She is an immigrant from the former Soviet Union, and she asks me a question new in my experience. As a result of the Soviet effort to stamp out every trace of Judaism, her father has never received a Jewish name. She inquires as to what it should be. I ask her, "What is his name?" She says, "Emile," which is close to "Emil," and I shoot back, "Yerachmiel." Unwittingly, a non-Jewish immigration officer has enabled me to play a role, small, yet I feel meaningful, in the Jewish tale of faith and perseverance, hope and redemption despite all odds.

Three years have now gone by, and another mother speaks to me before the evening service is to begin. Her younger son, a 4-year old, had finally summoned the courage several days before to join his brother as a "junior ritual director" at Congregation Mishkan Tefila in Chestnut Hill, Massachusetts, where I play the senior role. Whenever present, young children are asked if they would like to announce the pages of the prayers. I lean over each time an announcement is to be made, whisper the page number into the child's ear, and then he or she calls it out to the members of the Minyan. We attribute great importance to this role of the junior ritual director. The children enjoy doing it. The parents overflow with pride, and the *daveners* (pray-ers) in attendance are tickled pink. Most strikingly, even mourners are

i

touched, and a smile comes to their faces, as this taste of life eases their confrontation with a loved one's death. And on the occasion in question, the mother turns to me and relates something her younger son had done the night before with the *Yad*, or Torah pointer, we give each of our junior ritual directors as a gift. He had taken it to bed and gone to sleep with it! In an endearing way this young fellow had expressed his sense of identification with the Torah and pride in being an agent of Jewish life.

My work as a ritual director was not planned from the start. I began my professional life teaching philosophy and Jewish thought at the high school and college levels, went on to work as a cantor and was then invited to assume a position in which all my interests and skills found expression. I could sing and instruct, *kibbitz* and console, write articles and sermonize. I could work with all age-groups and bring the light touch suitable to an "in the trenches" clergyman. As I once wrote,

> A ritual director is a spiritual jack-of-all-trades. He leads the Minyan and reads the Torah. He trains the kids and teaches the adults. He delivers a *Dvar[1]* dishes up a *Davening.[2]* He tells jokes to the saddened and gives solace to the broken-hearted. Clergyman and comedian, utility player and designated leader, he is both standard-bearer of tradition and jester in the courts of the righteous and the holy. Such is a ritual director in his manner and way.

As the above incidents make clear, being a ritual director has also taught me of the meaning to be found in concrete, down-to-earth experiences. Giving an individual a name may become an occasion for experiencing the eternity of the Jewish people. Dispensing the gift of a ritual object may become the channel through which I am touched by the glow of a child's love of Torah. And as for praying, twice a day I hang out not in some august forum, but in a chapel, a place of informality, where I direct services. Here one need not qualify for the Metropolitan Opera in order to lead the *davening*. Even if one's vocal

---

1   *Dvar Torah* is the fuller term and means a talk on a selection from the Torah.

2   Literally, praying; used to refer to the chanting and singing of the leader of a service.

ability falls short of that of a Pavarotti, a sincerity still pulsates in the chant of the congregants, and many a soul in grief has been healed by the naturalness and humanness of our homey sacred space.

During my tenure as ritual director, I have not lost the passion I feel in grappling philosophically with the great questions of human and Jewish existence. What is the nature of God? What is the significance of human beings, who are part of the biological realm and yet have a craving for spiritual meaning? May we human beings go beyond outer appearances and have a direct, soul-to-soul contact with each other? May we sense something eternal in the path we share with other Jews, in life itself, in our being as individuals? These questions stir me, and my concern with them is evident, I believe, in the pages that follow. But my method is not that of overt philosophical argumentation. In this book you will find articles from the synagogue bulletin, written in the offbeat style I enjoy as the "Mishkan Tefila Cowboy" (the title given me by a student in a course in which I compared our rambunctious Biblical ancestors to cowboys of the Wild West). You will find commentary on Torah and liturgy, mixed with humor and anecdote. You will find sermonic reflection, bolstered by references to both the literary and the commonplace.[3] With "straight talk" you will discover the funny (or at least efforts in that direction) and the tongue-in-cheek. Our ancestor Isaac may not have had the happiest of lives. But his name still means "he shall laugh." So, who are we to be morose, stuck in the mud of conventional speech, fearful of joy as a token of illumination?

In my work as Mishkan Tefila ritual director I have been taught by life, an accomplishment (a miracle?) for one deeply engrossed in the world of thought. Here in the immediate and the down-to-earth I have been touched by that light which may truly shine within the everyday. In relating stories from life, in reflecting on texts and tales from our tradition, in *kibbitzing*, sermonizing and commenting on everything from Darwin and the Lubavitcher Rebbe to Hank Greenberg and Jewish spirituality, I hope that I perk up your spirit and add bounce to your soul. In speaking from my humble position within the maelstrom of a people's life perhaps I can also address that which stirs within

---

3   The sermon on Parshat Bo, "From Slavery to Light," first appeared in *The American Rabbi*, Vol. 25, No. 3, December, 1992.

your heart and give it my own idiosyncratic, yet hopefully faithful, expression.

A synagogue, a *shul*, we call in Hebrew a *beit kenesset*, or house of assembly. In this milieu we may taste—and must certainly try to nurture—that connectedness which is itself part of the salvation people seek. In this milieu we may give expression to those spiritual urges which so often remain unvoiced and unrealized in our society, in which technology has not meant tranquillity and the "mad rush" has not given the peace of Shabbat.

Let us discover that life need not be a frenetic search after fleeting pleasures, but that through a concrete spiritual path we may find an inner peace, born of the sense that we are not lonely denizens of a meaningless world. To the contrary, we derive from a spiritual source, whom we seek and who we discover to be our abiding home. You can come home again. For home, notwithstanding the pain we encounter in this world, is where you are.

And so, I would suggest, when you read of Mishkan Tefila in this book you need not think only of the synagogue in Chestnut Hill, Mass., where I serve as ritual director. Rather this synagogue, whose name is inspired by the original sanctuary of the Jewish people, the Mishkan or tabernacle in the Wilderness of Sinai, may also be regarded as a symbol of every synagogue.

For every synagogue may be a Mishkan for Tefila, a sanctuary for prayer, giving us a sense of God's presence in our midst, of God being, if you wish, the very place or home where we are.

Bon appetit, my friend. May the words which follow both touch your heart and gladden your soul. May they stir and reinforce in you a path which has been preserved for this generation—and beyond.

Dr. Davin Wolok
January, 2010

ACKNOWLEDGMENTS

Appreciation is due for their help in the writing of this book first to my wife, Carol, and our daughter, Rina. The emotionally and intellectually stimulating environment which they helped shape became the soil in which the impulse to create took root. The tossing around of ideas, the banter, the joy in conversation, the love I felt—and hopefully gave—became the context in which the desire to communicate in print grew. With them self-expression was experienced as a form of sharing. To Carol and Rina I offer my boundless gratitude.

Thanks are due also to both the colleagues and congregants I have met at Congregation Mishkan Tefila. They have provided me with an arena in which I find professional fulfillment, while experiencing and participating in the life of a community. Their openness to and affirmation of my efforts at creative expression are deeply appreciated. Mention should be made of two past presidents, Dr. Barry Benjamin, who recommended that I publish a collection of my synagogue bulletin articles, and Mr. Stephen Samuels, who encouraged me to publish my sermons. Their support is characteristic of the entire congregation.

To my parents, Emil and Shoshana Wolok, to my siblings, Debby and Phil, to my teachers from my early years through graduate school and to my friends I express my heartfelt thanks. They all contributed centrally to the intellectual-spiritual milieu, both Jewish and general, from which I derive and to which I have responded. Experiences long past have a living presence, and memories of "way back when" reveal influences which reverberate still in soul and deed.

To Rabbi Gilbert Rosenthal I express my gratitude for his insightful comments regarding both the content of the book and the form of its presentation.

To my friend, Harvey Sukenic, the librarian of the Hebrew College of Greater Boston, I offer my thanks for proofreading the book and providing invaluable recommendations toward its improvement.

To Mel Levine, my friend and fellow member of the Mishkan Tefila community, I offer my thanks both for his generosity in support of my work and for his spiritual example. When Lenny Florence,

Mel's friend for whom he had worked, died, Mel, despite the absence of any religious obligation, came to our services for eleven months, reciting Kaddish in memory of a man he could never forget. His devotion is an inspiration.

Finally, to my brother-in-law Martin Lurie, and to my friend Isaac Sadovnik I express my appreciation for assistance in navigating the world of computers and formatting the text. Their tireless efforts on behalf of my project and their zest in enabling me to progress are memorable. For a person who only several years ago said, "For me a ballpoint pen is advanced technology," their help was both essential and irreplaceable.

Davin Wolok

Part I

*FROM HANK GREENBERG TO THE
WILD WEST:
AN INVITATION TO LIFE AS A JEW*

Section I

MINYAN AND OPINION

"An All-Star Welcome to the Chapel"
"To Darwin and to Daven"
"Mysticism and Physics in the Mishkan Tefila Chapel"
"I Have a Dream?: Reflections on Sleepwalking and
Awakening"
"A Halakhic Question"
"Ten Questions"
"I Know There Are No Words:
Reflections on the Limitations of Human Speech"
An Advertisement and an Article:
"Time Shares—'It's Heavenly!'"
"You're Pulling My Leg... Oh, No I Ain't!"
"A Journey"

AN ALL-STAR WELCOME TO THE CHAPEL

My father and I were sitting on the third-base line at Tiger Stadium, and a man was on second from the visiting team. The pitch came in, and the batter whacked the ball to deep right, all the way to the warning track. My childhood hero, Al Kaline, went back, caught the ball and fired a strike to the belly of the third baseman. He didn't, however, catch the runner on a slide into third, as the man, seeing Kaline's throw, returned to second after venturing only a short way off the bag.

The memory came back to me, by association, when I was recently reading a book loaned to me by Brotherhood Executive Vice-President and Minyan Booster, Chuck Diamond. It is entitled *Hank Greenberg: The Story of My Life* and deals with a Tiger great which not I, but my father, was fortunate to see play.

Greenberg established himself as a hero to the Jews of Detroit not only because of his play on the field, but also because of his performance outside of Tiger Stadium one day in 1934. It was late in the season, and the Tigers had just about sewn up the American League pennant race.

But when the game of Sept. 18, that year, rolled around, Greenberg was not giving an accounting of himself on the diamond, but in a synagogue, before God, on Yom Kippur. The proud and enthusiastic reaction Greenberg received from his fellow congregants upon entering the shul is related in his autobiography.

"On Yom Kippur, my friends, a family named Allen, took me to shul. We walked in about 10:30 in the morning and the place was jammed.... Right in the middle of everything, everything seemed to stop.... suddenly everybody was applauding. I was embarrassed; I didn't know what to do. It was a tremendous ovation for a kid who was only twenty-three years old, and in a synagogue, no less!"

I am proud to say that the synagogue into which Greenberg strode that day was the one of my youth, Congregation Shaarey Zedek.

Now we do not yet give ovations in the chapel of Mishkan Tefila to those who come in to participate in daily services. But the heartiness and enthusiasm with which worshipers are greeted on a regular basis would, I believe, elicit the same good feeling which Hank Greenberg felt that day in Detroit. It is not a one-time deal. It is an everyday practice.

Experience the comradery of daily services at Mishkan Tefila. Join us morning or eve, and receive *an ongoing all-star welcome to the chapel.*

TO DARWIN AND TO DAVEN

I entered the building of my childhood shul and headed down the hall toward my Hebrew high teacher, Dov Parshan. Mr. Parshan was a follower of the Rabbi Menachem Mendel Schneersohn, the rebbe, or revered spiritual leader, of the Lubavitcher Hassidim. He had given me an article by the rebbe "disproving evolution," and I knew he would want to know what I thought.

When we met, he asked, "Did you read the article?," and I said that, yes, I had. He then asked, "Did you understand the article?," and I said that, yes, I did. He finally asked, "Do you believe the article?," and I said that, no, I did not. To which he responded, "Then you don't understand the article."

Now we can surmise that Mr. Parshan had a predisposition to accept what Rabbi Schneershon said. But it is striking that we, too, feel gripped by the Torah in a special, even if not always literal, way. From it we gain not knowledge of the evolution of species, but a sense of the wonder and transcendent meaningfulness of all life. Genesis, read as spiritual poetry, confirms our feeling that the birth of every child, even though it involves no deviation from the laws of nature, is still a miracle.

To provide only one example: During the period of gestation the placenta forms, by means of which the fetus is fed. After the birth of the child, the placenta, no longer needed, exits the mother's body. Now imagine, by analogy, that you are placed for a nine-month period in an empty room, and soon after your entrance a self-powered and fully-stocked refrigerator rolls in, from which you nourish yourself. After nine months you are allowed out of the room, and suddenly, right after you leave, so does the refrigerator.

Would this not cause you to wonder what was going on? Perhaps a purely natural explanation accounts for the behavior of the refrigerator. But then, wouldn't the existence of this explanation cause you wonderment? Science points to facts. But the facts point to more.

And here is one fact, conveyed to me by an old friend, that really makes me wonder. Once, driving out in the country, he saw a little monkey run across the road, not far ahead of where he was. He stopped and suddenly an older monkey darted across the road, picked up the "kid," put it over her knee—and spanked it! These must have been members of a *monkey mishpocheh!* So, evolution involves not just competition, but a sense of kinship and connectedness as well.

Did an elementary school science teacher sense my special interest in evolution when she once called me "Darwin" rather than "Davin"? Perhaps she also sensed that I could affirm the value of our scientific quest, while experiencing Rabbi Schneersohn's love of Torah.

It may not be such a shame to be descended from a monkey. In the Psalms we read, "Everything which breathes shall praise God." Who knows? If we look we may find that our "ancestors" *daven* in a Minyan of their own. As a *Davin* I would be gratified... just as I would be to greet you in our own *Chapel for Homo Sapiens!*

See you, God willing, soon.

MYSTICISM AND PHYSICS
IN THE MISHKAN TEFILA CHAPEL

Some years ago at Columbia University I heard Elie Wiesel speak on the topic of Soviet Jewry. Both his content and his delivery made an indelible impression on me. First, the latter. Wiesel spoke in a very soft voice, almost a whisper, and yet, amazingly enough, was heard throughout the auditorium. I was sitting in the balcony, but may as well have been across a desk. It was as if there was a stillness more still than usual, as if the room were filled with a palpable quiet, through which his voice penetrated without any interference. And the message he conveyed was an urgent and heartfelt one, that of the need of Soviet Jewry for support and salvation.

In the course of his talk, Wiesel related the story of an unusual event which took place in Moscow during the Six Day War. Each day Jews filled a synagogue, and even after the time for prayer concluded, would continue to sit, inwardly meditating, praying for their sisters and brothers in the Land of Israel. They were observed by an agent of the government, but they would not budge. Although distant from the scene of difficulty, distress and war, they felt bound to the fellow members of their extended family, the Jewish people. And it was Wiesel's view, his mystical view, that in some way reaching beyond our rational comprehension, these Soviet Jews, in fact, contributed to the victory of Israel. Did he mean that their support was, as it were, telepathically conveyed, working within the Israelis, whether or not they consciously picked up the "signal" from Moscow?

When I think of this aspect of Wiesel's talk, I am reminded of a topic which has caught the fancy of one of our members, Alan Axelrod, who now lives in Hawaii. A physics buff, Alan discussed with me on a recent trip the scientific concept of "entangled particles." If two particles have interacted, then even when they are at a tremendous distance, they act in sync, one, as it were, adjusting its behavior to that of the other. They are too far from each other for one to "know" what the other is doing. But they act as if they are in immediate contact. Was Wiesel perhaps speaking not of "entangled particles,"

9

but of "entangled souls"? And what might this have to do with us at Mishkan Tefila?

In response to the crisis facing our people in Israel, we in the chapel have adopted the policy of concluding each morning and evening service with the recitation of the prayer for the State of Israel and the singing of Hatikvah. Certainly, it is important that we continually remind ourselves of our brothers and sisters to whom we are bound heart and soul. Certainly, we need to give voice to our anguish, our hope, our concern and our faith. Certainly, we need to reinvigorate ourselves so that we speak out and act when we leave the chapel, when we address ourselves to neighbors, to the press and to government leadership.

But even if it is only a possibility, even if it cannot be known for sure, perhaps somehow the call of our heart does not remain within, but is transmitted from innermost soul to innermost soul, to our fellow Jews in Israel.

Entangled particles? Entangled souls? The Minyan is an island of fellowship and support, which is not, however, an island unto itself. Come to the Mishkan Tefila chapel and experience your fellowship with the worldwide family, the worldwide community, of People Israel.

I HAVE A DREAM?
Reflections on Sleepwalking and Awakening

I was a university student at the time and for some reason had a hard time making it to a course I liked as often as one would expect. I don't know exactly what caused it. First, this would come up and then—that. In fact, there was a whole group of us who, though liking the course, so often found it difficult to attend that one day the professor read our names aloud and said that if any of us missed even one more time, he would be out of the class.

Not being intentionally in violation of the course attendance requirement, I took to heart the professor's warning. Yet, shortly afterward I had the following strange experience. I went to sleep one night, and for some reason slept and slept and slept. I was sure I had set the alarm the night before, but when the dream ended, I awoke to see the clock read "4:00 P.M." The class was given in the morning, and I thought, boy, am I kaput. There's no way out of this one.

But suddenly, I woke up! It had been a dream. I mean I hadn't really woken up when I thought I did. I was still asleep. I was dreaming of waking up. But I really hadn't. Now that I was awake and could see it was early, I was saved. I wasn't booted out of the class—though on a later occasion, I must confess, I came pretty close.

Now what is the meaning of this unforgettable experience— unforgettable at least in a state of waking consciousness? Was it simply that I was anxiety-ridden and imagined—or dreamt—the worst? This surely is part of the picture. But there might also be another lesson, a symbolic one, in the fact that I didn't immediately wake up following the original dream. And that is that waking up is not always easy.

Physically? Do I mean that getting up out of bed is a pain when you're still tired and want to rest? No. For to be at that point you must have already woken up. I mean something else. I mean something that can occur when you're already awake in the normal sense, and that is being unaware of, *asleep to* an issue which might be uncomfortable to think about. I mean being forgetful of or *asleep to* something whose

11

recognition might jar your normal way of thinking and feeling and functioning.

Our late president, John Kennedy, wrote a book entitled, *Why England Slept*, describing the wish of the British to look away from the danger which Germany posed to them during the years preceding World War II. Presumably, the Brits were awake, going about their daily tasks without the appearance of being sleepwalkers. And yet, in a real—and tragic—sense they were asleep. The truth of Germany's growing threat was there for all to see. But there had to be the willingness to see—that is, to see something staring them in the face.

Not all cases of what we may call waking sleep are explainable as the product of fear. Some may simply come out of habit. Living in a culture which puts pressure on us to function at a frantic pace, we may become dishabituated to thinking about and feeling those things of which we become aware only when we slow down. We may come to place less value on those things. We may even come to place less value on the experience of slowing down, being at peace, ceasing to accomplish for the sake of feeling at one—with ourselves, with others and with the spiritual dimension of life.

I am constantly struck by the powerful impact of the daily Minyan on those who give themselves a chance and attend. Often this occurs when people have lost a loved one. Our tradition encourages them to take time out each day, to be with others in a homey, warm setting, to pray and reflect, to chat, to converse, to lend and receive a consoling word.

Others not in a period of mourning form part of our crew of regulars. I know that enabling there to be a Minyan for those reciting Kaddish is one of their concerns. But they, too, get something irreplaceable out of their participation—an experience of community, a feeling of peace and a sense of life as a spiritually meaningful enterprise, not one dominated only by competition and the drive to "succeed."

How do you convince someone in a fast mode that the slow mode also has its pleasures, its fulfillment and its satisfactions? To those used to rock, it must seem like an outmoded fox trot. Does it even receive enough conscious attention to be consciously rejected?

As I complete these reflections or ruminations, I glance over at my clock and see that it is 4:00 P.M. Am I perchance still sleeping? I seem to recall a morning service in which I participated, but was that, too, a dream? If not, will my words, composed in waking reality, reach those for whom they are intended? I can't shake them to find out if they are in a listening mode. But are they?

Perhaps in the rush, the appeal of rest, of rest and spiritual refreshment, will also be heard — and connect.

A HALAKHIC QUESTION

It was 2058 in the Gregorian calendar, and on the first day of Nissan (the month of our liberation from Egypt), 5818 in the Jewish calendar, Samuel found himself alone in the Mishkan Tefila chapel. The time for services had already come and gone, but no one else had arrived. What was permitted halakhically (i.e., according to Jewish law)? Could he use the recently developed technology to instantaneously clone nine copies of himself and thereby have a Minyan in which to daven? Or would he have to wait for nine biologically conceived cohorts in order to engage in communal worship of the Almighty?

Jewish legal codes of his time had not yet rendered an opinion on this vexing question. Yet, Samuel did not feel that he was without recourse in finding an answer. For precognition (seeing into the future) was an already established epistemological methodology (technique for knowing) and Samuel realized that he could make a mental leap forward and peruse the discussions of Halakhic experts who would wrestle with this question in time to come.

Examining a text called *Biotechnology and Communal Prayer*, Samuel peeked into an argument advanced by Reb David Bohm, great-grandson of the renowned twentieth-century quantum physicist of the same name. Drawing on an ancient Midrash, Bohm noted that each individual human being is unique and in this way created in the very image of the Almighty, who is only one and therefore, by definition, unique. Thus, to count as a human being you would have to be unique. Wouldn't that rule out clones? Still as Bohm's great-granddad had noted, everything in the universe is unique. Even every particle is unique. Two electrons might seem identical to us. But the history of their interactions with other particles could not be absolutely the same. This one might have bounced up against a flower, and this one against a rock. The impact of these different collisions would result in subtle differences between the electrons. Perhaps we could not detect them. But they must be there. Therefore clones, which are composed of particles, cannot be truly identical and they should each count as a human being. Cloning, thus, could produce a Minyan.

Yet, Reb Bohm continued, to be a genuine Yid (or Jew), your

14

mother had to be a flesh-and-blood Jew. Even if clones could be Yiddin (Jews), how could they come from a man? Halakhically speaking, Samuel was still in a bind. Still, Reb Bohm noted, the first person to give birth, according to the Torah, was a man, namely Adam, from whom a rib was extracted in the creation of Eve. So, if you're in a tight spot, perhaps a man could qualify as a mother and, thus, give birth to a Minyan.

Breathing a sigh of relief, Samuel pulled out his cloning kit, ready to manufacture his own Minyan. Suddenly he heard a voice from heaven cry out, "Samuel, this is Me, and if you think you're hallucinating, watch what I'm gonna do." Immediately, the chapel began to whirl around like a spinning dreidel. Samuel's consciousness was swishing from side to side. He couldn't take it and screamed, "Stop, I'll do whatever you say." At which point the Almighty said in no uncertain terms, "I ain't interested in all your fancy Minyan technology. I am the God of the heart. I am the God of the soul. Tell your buddies there are no cop-outs. There are no easy routes. Fulfillment will be theirs, but only when they take the step themselves. In coming you have already fulfilled a Mitzvah. I am waiting for all and will always keep the door open."

Samuel was shocked, but relieved at being at being able to stand straight, without his mind gyrating 'round and 'round. Was there hope?, he wondered. In an age of technological link-ups and virtuality, will people come together in the flesh and meet face to face? Will they address their Creator together in person?

Employing his powers of retrocognition (direct perception of the past), Samuel sought to discover what steps were taken in an earlier phase to stem the tide toward Minyan diminution. A view of a half-century before slowly came into view.

Who knows? Perhaps Samuel is looking at us now. What will we show him? Can we perhaps make his present—future to us—but a fantasy, not a fact?

The answer lies in the heart—and will—of each of you. May we all act with the wisdom which hindsight would impart.

TEN QUESTIONS

1. Of late we have done better with the Minyan at Mishkan Tefila. But to meet all contingencies, should we not reflect further? And so ...

2. Are there any reminders, immediately available, which can trigger desire to attend the Minyan? Ten fingers? Ten toes? Converting to the metric system?

3. If a Minyan cannot be formed, but nine people assemble for a baseball team, may they open the ark and be counted as a Minyan?

4. If eleven people compose a football team, may one go out to make coffee, while the other ten *daven*? A Minyan, *n'est-ce pas*?

5. Five people play on a basketball team. But if two teams compete ... PRESTO! A MINYAN???

6. On Shabbat, the sages say, we each gain an extra soul. If half a Minyan shows up, should we multiply five bodies by two souls each to reach the required quorum of ten?

7. On Passover we read of the wise son, the wicked son, the simple son and the son who can't come up with a question. If ten wicked sons suddenly show up for Minyan, just to tease the righteous who don't, does their insincere deed make *them* righteous?

8. If a Minyan dies, who says Kaddish for it?

9. Can the Kaddish say Kaddish for a Minyan? Perhaps it is not possible. But is it permitted?

10. Is writing questioning articles the way to encourage people to come to the Minyan? Do you have the answer? Or the question? Pray, tell me.

Davin Wolok, Mishkan Tefila Ritual Director and Disciple to Rabbi Yitzchak ibn Badchan, Spiritual Leader of Congregation Beit Borschtbelt and Editor of MINYAN AND OPINION: A JOURNAL OF COMEDIC COMMENTARY AND IRONIC INTERPRETATION.

"I KNOW THERE ARE NO WORDS"
Reflections on the Limitations of Human Speech

Yesterday I visited a friend, a man fifty-six years old, who has suffered from a stroke, leaving him largely speechless. The topic on which I am about to write would certainly be inappropriate, if addressed to him. He no doubt fervently wishes to regain the capacity for speech, a capacity which in his case stood far beyond the norm, as did the thoughts gaining expression through it.

Words we value in Judaism. God, we say, created the world through speech. Words of kindness, we stress, bear the power to uplift and to heal. And a teaching uttered to one in youth may open a mind for the entire duration of a life. Finally—or perhaps firstly—words are a means of being together with others, of bonding with them, of drawing them into the circle of our interest and concern.

But notwithstanding the crucial importance of words, notwithstanding their painful lack in one such as my friend—and tragically many others—there is something which words cannot do. There is something that words, if we rely on them alone, cannot do. And that is to allow us to taste that which is unspoken, or "in other words"—silence.

When writing about the Minyan, I have often, as you know, stressed the conviviality which you will experience when you come. That is certainly true and of paramount importance. Minyanaires, both mourners and otherwise, turn toward each other in conversation, offering consolation, making the other feel, "You are not alone."

When meeting those in the early stages of grief, they do not pretend to have the magical words which will dispel the pain of loss. The sentiment which, in fact, seems to get expressed is, "I know there are no words. I just want to say I am here." One's presence, one's silent presence, sends a message which surpasses that which is contained within utterance.

This notion, that silence need not be an uncomfortable emptiness to be filled up with chatter, is the other side of the coin from the emphasis upon speech within Judaism. In the Torah God reveals Himself through Ten Declarations, or Commandments, issued amidst thunder and lightning and the quaking of Mount Sinai. But when revealing Himself to the prophet, Elijah, God makes it clear that He may be experienced through the "sound" of a "gentle silence." As everything quiets down outside, one may find oneself within a stillness which seems laden with meaning, even though we have no words to describe it.

If you're wondering what I mean, think of when you look at a sleeping baby in a crib. Their screaming and crying and squealing and cooing have ended, and while they're doing "nothing," you can gaze and gaze and gaze. It's all so meaningful—yet the meaning cannot be verbalized. The notion advanced by some philosophers that life is absurd would itself seem absurd at that moment.

The Minyan is not only a place for words, those of prayer and those of conversation. The Minyan is also a place where we can silently be together. The Minyan is also a place where you don't have to "perform," having the right word to say, constantly having to respond. You can be silent. You can simply—be.

And so, I would like to close this article by giving you an opportunity to think, to reflect, to let peace descend into your mind and soul for a brief duration and hopefully more. Here goes.

All the best to you in speech—and in silence.

TIME SHARES—"THEY'RE HEAVENLY!"

It's time for me to 'fess up. Ever since I became the ritual director of Mishkan Tefila, I've dreamt of running a business in the chapel, an operation that would bring in more people by offering something, you know, irresistible.

We don't deal with the ephemeral. We don't deal with the passing. We deal with what is everlasting in importance, with spiritual meaning and the sense of community which involves Jews and the whole human race worldwide, not only today, but yesterday and, God willing, tomorrow. We direct ourselves to the Source of the Whole Show and turn our thoughts to loved ones who are gone through the recitation of the Kaddish.

We deal with the big stuff, and so, it seemed obvious: I needed to offer a product which was eternal in its wallop. I needed to offer something simply heavenly. Time shares, I thought. Time shares in the next world. That was a product which couldn't be beat. With a product like that (renewable for free), people would come flocking to the Minyan.

Who ever heard of such a deal? All you do is show up and you receive a coupon that is your passageway to life eternal. They'll be beating down the doors. The walls will burst.

People will flock to get this product of which generations have dreamt. Just come. If you don't know how to put on Tefillin, no sweat. We'll help you. And if you decide to remain Tefillin-less, that will be no impediment.

You can't read Hebrew? That's okay. There are transliterations. And in any case, silent meditation will do. It's all so easy. Just show up—and you're in.

Well, as you can see from the ad I've placed, I kinda took the step—and then drew back. I made like it was a big joke, like I was only kidding when I said, "In all seriousness," intimating that the ad was a put on, a come on, a lure for a cure that I couldn't deliver.

But then I got to thinking and realized that it wasn't such a joke, that even as it stood it was for real. And the answer was in the Siddur, the prayer book, itself. Because we have one prayer which is pretty strange when you stop to think about it and ask what it really means. It is recited after a portion of the Torah is read and goes like this:

"Praised are You, O Sovereign, our God, King Eternal, who has given us a Torah of truth and planted eternal life amidst us. Praised are You, Who gives Torah."

That's strange, isn't it? How in the world can God plant eternal life "amidst us" right now, here and now? Doesn't eternal life come only, God willing, after or when our earthly journey is done?

No, it's not so strange. It really isn't. What the prayer means is that right now, here and now, we can taste something that matches the very definition of eternal life. Life eternal in Judaism doesn't just mean life that goes on forever. It means life which is characterized by that which is eternal in value, by fellowship and friendship and love, by the feeling of meaning which comes from the sense of God's presence, a presence, I might add, which is felt not only in moments of mystic exaltation.

As Solomon says in the Book of Proverbs, "a candle of the Lord is the human soul." In encountering a fellow human being, we meet not simply a complicated biological organism, but a being of infinite value, a living allusion to his or her own Divine Source. We meet one whose worth is not a function of social status, but an endowment of the Creator of all.

By coming to the Minyan you will get time shares in the next world—time shares that may be tasted in the here and now! Taste the peace which comes from participation in a community where you don't have to perform in order to be valued. Experience the fulfillment that comes from fellowship for its own sake. Partake of the connectedness that comes when your thoughts are turned both to your ancestors and departed loved ones and to new generations, both born and unborn. Feel the inner quiet that comes from the faith that there is One who is watching and who cares.

To such a life, to such a life eternal here and now, we are often asleep. But to it we may awake.

So, I'm not kidding, folks. I have a business in the chapel and I deal in time shares. When you come to the Minyan and partake of our *time of sharing*, you will taste something everlasting in quality and value.

The taste test is free.

The payoff is eternal.

"YOU'RE PULLING MY LEG... OH, NO I AIN'T"

We were looking for 76 West, the last major road taking us to Beaver Run, the residential school for developmentally disabled children where our daughter, Rina, is working this year. We drove and drove and drove, finally pulling off the road at a rest stop, where we asked a friendly gentleman for directions. He said we were already on 76 West, but had driven beyond our exit. "But there was no sign," we said. "Welcome to Pennsylvania," he answered. We decided to proceed to our hotel, check in, then swing back through beautiful farmland to Beaver Run.

What occurred afterwards was a dream. Or at least it's hard to convince myself that it wasn't. For what we beheld and tasted at Beaver Run was the realization of spiritual ideals so often proclaimed, but seldom brought to fruition. I am not suggesting that at Beaver Run we witnessed the perfect achievement of utopia. But what we did encounter was a genuine commitment to the inestimable value of each individual, a conviction that meaning is found in life when our concern is for the other and not only the self, and a sense that whatever our condition, fortunate or not, we as humans are a fellowship of spiritual equals. The helper also needs and is helped by the one she helps.

Beaver Run is part of an international network of live-in settings for developmentally disabled individuals that goes under the name Camphill, and is itself also known as the Camphill Special School. All of the Camphill settings are designed for the benefit of those suffering from severe learning disabilities. A walk to the woods abutting Beaver Run took us to the Soltane Camphill, for adults age 18-25. Twenty minutes away is the Kimberton Camphill, where adults of any age may live.

Carol's and my big introduction to Beaver Run came in the lobby of the school building, near both classrooms and the meeting hall where we would hear a beautiful concert during our stay. What immediately struck us was the vitality and aliveness of the children, the unabashed way in which they gave expression to their own individuality. Strangely enough—or perhaps not so strangely—they seemed more their natural selves than many in general society. I do not want to romanticize, but notwithstanding their difficulties—or even through them—they came across powerfully as authentic and highly appealing personalities. In their presence one felt both saddened and uplifted, the former because of their plight, the latter because that was clearly not the last word.

One of our most touching moments was during the word group Rina ran, when the kids were asked to read or write specific words. At one point, Sammy, sitting opposite us, said, "You're pulling my leg." When he saw that we got a kick out of his saying this, he, every minute or so, kept repeating the line, with his voice rising at the end. Two days later, at the concert, when Sammy saw us, he turned and said once again, "You're pulling my leg," and the smiles once more flashed in both directions.

Then there was Margaret, who is deaf and has never learned to speak. Her ebullience and the sincerity when she looks in your eyes reach directly into your innermost self. As our tradition teaches, "What comes from the heart enters the heart."

The essence of the Camphill philosophy is that the spirit within, notwithstanding all difficulties, remains wholly intact. The instrument through which it must express itself may not be whole. But the spirit, the person in his or her essence, is more than the instrument.

As a Jew, it was not lost on me that the coworkers of Camphill (this is the egalitarian term for both short- and long-term staff) are teaching and supporting and nurturing those who, alongside us, were murdered by the Nazis during World War II. Nor did it escape me that Viktor Frankl, the great Jewish psychiatrist who survived Auschwitz, felt similarly called to emphasize the ultimate spiritual integrity and dignity of every person, notwithstanding his difficulties. If a person is tied in knots, is the person only the knots?

Finally, I must note the pragmatic benefits of the moral philosophy shared by Camphill and Frankl. Regarding people as spiritual beings embodied, but not only their bodies, one comes to see them and act toward them in a new way. One comes to experience them in a new way. One feels poignantly how they may also touch one and help one.

Spirituality is not a peripheral need in life. It is at the core. It is not a dimension alongside others. It permeates them all. Thus, for example, social relation becomes what it is meant to be when the other is experienced not only as one we enjoy being with, but also—or even first and foremost—as one to whom we must respond. And I should add, we may respond simply by being there, as in a Shiva, where our presence, more than our words, is what counts most.

So, in this spirit I again invite you to participate and partake in our chapel Minyan services. Whether you meet mourners, Yahrzeit observers or simply fellow congregants and members of the community who have come to pray, you, by your presence, will lift them up.

In closing, let me say that you may think I'm exaggerating in pushing the benefits on the Minyan. Perhaps like Sammy you will say, "You're pulling my leg." But I ain't! The fellowship you will taste when you come will feel like fulfillment itself.

To paraphrase the German-Jewish philosopher Martin Buber, we become what we are, children of God, by becoming what we are, brothers of our brothers.

And as always, the time is—now.

A JOURNEY

The following story is told me by Arnon Ben Shlomo, director of the Ulpan conversational program at the Boston Hebrew College in the 1980s. One night the father of a friend of his awoke with a startle, feeling that he had received a blow to his shoulder. There was no one else in the room, except his sleeping wife, and he had not had a dream in which people were fighting or struggling. But immediately the man felt that his son was in danger. He searched and finally found him in a military hospital, having been struck by a bullet in the shoulder, exactly where his father had experienced a blow. The son's brush with death had occurred on the Sinai front, during the opening hours of the 1973 Yom Kippur War.

Now not all experiences of human interconnectedness are quite as extraordinary as that of Arnon's friend and his father. But as we get older the feeling, God willing, grows that we are not on purely individual journeys in life, but are rather participants in a story larger than ourselves, one whose full meaning and significance we grasp only in part. This feeling, of participating in something greater, seems to redeem us, to make us feel that we have a purpose transcending the private goals we have set for ourselves.

In this vein, the novelist, Kurt Vonnegut, created the concept of the karass, by which he meant a group we do not voluntarily choose to join, but which is still comprised of individuals with whom our lives are meaningfully intertwined. We may not know all the members of our karass—even who they are. Yet, they, too, count as participants in what is ultimately an instrument of divine providence in the world. They, too, help to realize the dimly glimpsed purpose for the sake of which the karass exists.

Last Thursday, as Shabbat Yitro (when the Ten Commandments are read) was approaching, I set off on an Amtrak train for Ann Arbor, Michigan, where Allen Elbaum, son of my friends Danny and Mary, was about to become Bar Mitzvah. Originally, I had thought that a train trip would be fun, more relaxing than a time-saving plane ride. I could read, see the countryside, get up and walk around when I liked, and in general enjoy an escape from the frantic pace of contemporary life. Briefly, however, my common sense got the best of me, and I attempted to switch to a round trip by the air. As luck would have it, I succeeded only in arranging a flight back. There was no flight that could get me to Detroit Metro, the closest airport to Ann Arbor, in time for Shabbat.

So, here I was, stepping into an Amtrak train, looking forward to a twenty-one hour journey to my Midwest destination. I climbed over the young man in an aisle seat, with briefcase in hand, ready to read and write and sleep. But he was a pretty friendly guy, and we got to talking. His name was Tim, and he said he was a soldier in the U.S. Army, off to see his girlfriend in Rochester, New York. I mentioned the name of our own Mishkan Tefila Dr. Abraham Zimelman, who heads the medical system for the Massachusetts National Guard, and Tim said that he had heard of him. With Tim, across the aisle and one row back, was Will, who was off to do something, I can't quite remember what. They asked what I did, and I tried to explain it as well as I could to these two young men of Christian background. Will, a Roman Catholic said, "Oh, you're a deacon."

Across from Tim and in front of Will was a man in his late thirties or early forties, who had put in two decades of service with the Marines. In front of him were two young women, both of whom had served in the military. They were friends, and one was a mother who had a child with her. The other also participated in taking care of the kid. Unfortunately, Will, who was a very engaging individual, got off the train after a few stops. That left the four present or past military people and—your deacon!

What was amazing was how this accidental assemblage of strangers, except for the two women, somehow jelled into a group of laughing, chatting friends, the kind you might think had known each other for years. Adding to the unexpected joy of this journey by train was the ticket collector, who, though he knew he might be without a job by the coming week, kept kibbitzing around and livening up the scene. Incidentally, the stub he had placed over my seat said "Toledo" and not "Ann Arbor," as the journey to Michigan stopped in Ohio, where Amtrak took you the rest of the way on one of its buses.

In addition to the high spirits, there were also moments both touching and tender in nature. So, for example, at one point I looked down the aisle and saw two individuals, at least one of whom was deaf, talking to each other in sign language. Further down was a mother cradling her child and gently dancing with her. I felt that this was a scene for a writer to behold, though in reality we all have the ability to see what our writers attempt to evoke.

It would be relevant at this point to mention the woman who was sitting slightly in front of me. She was with her teenage daughter, but was a pretty energetic character herself. She showed me a disc she had cut of Motown music (perfect for me, a Detroit boy), and when she got up to walk down the aisle and looked at the stub over my seat, she read it, kiddingly perhaps, as "Tel Aviv." Then she said that Tel Aviv was in Turkey, but corrected herself to Israel.

Well, finally, we got to Tel Aviv... I mean, Toledo, and I stepped into the Amtrak station, only to see before me a family of Hassidim. No, not exactly Hassidim, but people who looked a lot like them, especially if you've seen Gene Wilder's film, "The Frisco Kid." Yes, they were Amish folk, as I confirmed when I spoke to them. I knew this would be an important piece of news for my daughter, Rina, who wants to be a farmer and regards the Amish discomfort with technology as the embodiment of human wisdom.

I asked the father what language they were speaking, and he said Pennsylvania Dutch. He somewhat apologetically explained that they had taken over this language and kind of just added in words from other languages. I told him that sounded like Yiddish.

When I arrived in Ann Arbor, Danny picked me up and took me back to his house. There he introduced me to his cousin, Pinchas, from Carmiel, Israel. I mentioned that my sister, Debby, had lived some years back in Carmiel, but it was clear that she had left the town before Pinchas and his family moved in. I later asked Pinchas if he knew my cousin-by-marriage, Joan Weisman, who also lived in Carmiel. He said, "No," but when he called his wife, he asked her if she knew Joan. The answer was yes. In fact, Joan had taught the oldest of their three daughters and was a close friend of Pinchas's wife. The contours of my karass were growing richer by the moment.

Later Danny took me over to the home of Rochel and Jeff Urist, friends who had graciously agreed to put me up. As soon as Jeff walked in, I said, "I've seen you before." It's not that I had met him. But it was clear that we had crossed paths, and in fact a late dear friend of mine from Ann Arbor had been a dear friend of his and Rochel's, as well. When I saw a photograph on their refrigerator of Jeff and another friend of his, I recognized the latter individual as a Camp Ramah staff member who had chastised me in my younger days for the rambunctious behavior that I found rather appealing at the time.

Well, finally that night we got to the Friday evening service, held at the beautiful University of Michigan Hillel, located exactly where the Hillel I had frequented had been. But mine was no longer there, replaced by this newer building in the very same place. Similarly, I looked across the street to where I had lived in a Jewish co-op called The Hebrew House. But it, too, was no longer there, replaced by a nicer building, I must agree. Death and resurrection twice over, you might say, in a small geographical radius.

The following morning Allen did a splendid job with all his chanting, speaking and Torah reading. His talk was quite striking, a discourse on angels, prompted by their appearance in the Haftarah, taken from the Book of Isaiah. The most interesting of these beings were the Ofanim, formed out of two wheels, one inside the other at right angles. With their unusual construction, these Ofanim, possessed of the ability to think and feel and move themselves, were more fascinating to me than any robots conceived of by modern souls. Allen's references to Maimonides I, as a student of philosophy, found quite interesting. His illuminating talk reminded me of our own Mishkan Tefila students!

Following the service I introduced myself to the spiritual leader of the Orthodox congregation, one Rabbi Glowgower, who proceeded to tell me that he was a fellow student at Brandeis with our own educational director, Dr. Stephen Simons. During lunch I looked over to the next table and saw a young woman, Michelle Sternthal, whom I remembered from Temple Shalom of Milton, where I had served as cantor. Her grandparents Murray and Elaine Reiser, are members of the shul, while Michelle is now a doctoral candidate at the University of Michigan. Michelle's parents, Elliot and Adriane Sternthal, I had seen at Congregation Beth El-Atereth Israel in Newton the week before for a talk by Rabbi Norman Lamm, the chancellor of Yeshiva University. Just last night I saw Adriane and Michelle's great-grandmother Sally Lakin at Mishkan Tefila, when they came in observance of a Yahrzeit.

And so it was, on and on. Links unexpected. Friends in common. A mentor of my friend's son who had studied with a colleague here in Chestnut Hill.

Dr. Phillip Weiss, the spiritual leader of Temple B'nai Brith of Somerville, once said that alienation in the modern world is the illusion that we are alienated. The truth of our interconnectedness we see in Judaism not only as a blessed fact of life, but as a goal to be cultivated. The very name of a Jewish house of worship, Beit Kenesset, which means, "House of Assembly," "House of Community," "House of Conviviality," makes this point. In coming to our services, in partaking of our classes, in participating in our programs, you will strengthen the karass of your life, which is the true place you dwell, in a network of human relationships.

All this, as people of faith, we believe has a deep significance. In cherishing and cultivating these relationships, in recognizing and feeling their sacredness, we experience life itself as a journey in meaning. We look forward to enthusiastically greeting you at Mishkan Tefila, an important station in your own journey, both personal and interwoven with others, already known and yet to be discovered.

Section II

KABALLAH AND CONFETTI

"The Mundane or the Miraculous?: On Purim, Providence and Your
Personal Self"
"Passover Confetti"
"Given the Boot":
An Episode from The Adventures of a Hebrew School Rebel
"The Sounds of Silence"
"Latkes for Pesach"
"Revealing Revelation:
The Case of the Junior Ritual Directors"

THE MUNDANE OR THE MIRACULOUS
On Purim, Providence and Your Personal Self

I took the risk. Last month I wrote about Kabbalah, or Jewish mysticism, and the worst did not happen. No one reported to me that my article was what I feared, incomprehensible gobbledygook or nonsense. Well, should I test your patience once more? This month I have chosen to write on two topics of religious philosophy, one perennial and the other Purim-ial. Let me begin with the latter.

The Megillah, as you know, is a rather amazing book. Here it is in the *Tanach*, or Hebrew Bible, and it not once mentions the "Author of the Whole Show," I mean, the Almighty. What kind of holy book is this? I can read *Harry Potter* with my daughter, as I do, and at least as of yet, I have not come across the Divine One. Would I expect to find *Harry Potter* in Holy Writ? Of course not. So, why the Megillah?

You know, the rabbis in the Talmud were clever thinkers, something like intellectual detectives. And they concluded that it is absolutely appropriate that the Megillah is in the Bible. For God, you see, does not always make a big, public "splash," as He did with the liberation from Egypt, striking our oppressors with plagues and drying the waters of the Red Sea. That is the God of Pesach. But in the Megillah we find the God of Purim, who works behind the scenes through his human representatives. Mordecai and Esther, in particular, are agents of the Divine Will, saving the Jewish people through their actions, which God motivates from His "hide-out in heaven." He is satisfied to see good results, not needing a blaring headline in the morning press or—scroll. This is providence "on the sly," a trait suitable at times to a force who is, in any case—invisible.

Well, so much for the Purim-ial. Now for the perennial. Do we anywhere else experience the presence of the spiritual in the everyday or mundane world? As you might expect, the answer is yes, and here it is, in the eyes of Judaism, in human beings themselves, not in how we always act, but in what we're made of, in what we ultimately are. For, says the Torah, a human being is created "in the image of God," and that, say the rabbis, involves our being a composite of both a body and a soul. A human being is not simply a complicated biological machine. A human being is imbued with a higher element, in the language of contemporary thinkers, a self which perceives the world about her and aspires for higher realities, for the good, the true and the beautiful. Each self or soul is further unique. She is in the words of *The Book of Proverbs*, "a candle of the Lord."

Interestingly, this spiritual outlook has been advanced by one of the foremost neuroscientists of our time, Sir John Eccles. Winner of the Nobel Prize, Eccles argues forcefully for the fact that a person is more than a body guided by a complex computer, called the brain. Rather the body and the brain are susceptible to guidance by the self, which itself cannot be explained by physical science. Affected by the body and brain, it is nevertheless more than what brain science describes. And it is in each instance, as our tradition affirms, unique.

How does this spiritual philosophy pertain to our life of worship here at Mishkan Tefila? The answer is simple. Philosophy is not meant to stay in our heads, but rather to be felt in our heart and realized in our actions and our relationships. And the "arena," the atmosphere, counts. When you come to the synagogue, not the least to the homey setting of the chapel, you are in a "space" where you and the others with you can relax and feel more easily the uniqueness of each person. Here you don't have to wear a mask for professional success. Here you can be *you*, and not a xerox copy of some formula for "making it big in the real world." Here you can cultivate that self to take out to the world and perhaps uplift it a bit.

There are those who say that a spiritual conception of the person is an illusion. One day people will be cloned, and then, indeed, it will be apparent that people are nothing more than biological machines. The physical explains it all. Once again, an answer comes from a scientist of philosophical depth. His name is Gustav Fechner, and he was the founder of psychophysics, the science which studies how we come to perceive the world in response to physical stimuli. Although his research went far beyond what we might realize from our everyday lives, examples from this sphere will make his general area of concern clear.

A loud alarm from our clock wakes us up. A person who speaks softly, but not too softly, may make himself heard. If the physical stimuli are right, we will hear or see or—whatever. But as the window which allows the light to pass through is not the same thing as the light itself, so, too, the body which allows us to hear or see is not the same thing as the self which consciously experiences hearing or seeing. Thus, for example, the eyes are not simply a camera for vision. Rather, "the eyes are the window of the soul." Look into that place and you behold a being of value and feeling, not simply a complex clod of biologically organized chemicals. Whether procreated or cloned, the body is fused with a non-physical element, a soul. The body, says Fechner, allows the soul to function in the physical world.

In the everyday world we encounter human beings created in the image of God, unique souls who are more than their bodies which grow and change. And in the everyday there may be at work a Hand who is invisible and who, in humility, allows us to fulfill His will through the decisions we ourselves make. Come to our Megillah readings show your appreciation to a God who is real, even if He is not "in your face."

Come to the chapel every week and partake of a warm atmosphere in the fellowship of those who are, like you, representatives of the "CEO of the Whole Show." *The soul you buoy up may also be your own.*

PASSOVER CONFETTI

My buddies and I scampered up to the balcony of our childhood shul, Congregation Shaarey Zedek of Detroit. It was Passover, and we were holding in our hands the special "bread" of the festival, the "bread of affliction"—or Matzah. Quickly we prepared for our exploit, whose goal was to instill both the excitement of "naughty behavior" (especially when performed by "good boys") and the thrill of evading apprehension by parental and synagogal authorities in pursuit.

Quietly we broke the Matzah into tiny bits, peering over the balcony railing to the praying congregants below. Now, mind you, we really were "model young men." Regular shul attendees, solid students in the religious school, participants, many of us, in an extracurricular cantorial program, we had a level of commitment in which we, and not only our mentors, took pride. But this day, this day, mind you, a spirit of frivolity seemed to invade our souls and thrust us into a rendezvous with inappropriate behavior.

The congregation was in the midst of Hallel, the special collection of Psalms recited on festival and new moon. And the Matzah was a-ready. And the music was a-soaring. Suddenly, suddenly, a hail of sacramental confetti rose over the worshippers below us and descended upon them, oh so gently, as we dashed off the balcony, eluding capture and cognition by responsible, adult authority and personage.

Now had we been caught, what could we have said? Could we have said that we had, in fact, performed a ritual, enabling the people to be physically adorned with a remembrance of the Exodus from Egypt? Could such an explanation have been believed, even if our motive in making it were but a wish to escape condemnation and punishment? Could it be seen as a legitimate description of what the people experienced—or might have experienced—even if our aim were but the performance of a prank, the enactment of a diversion from upright behavior and the "straight path"?

No, of course not! But why not? In all seriousness, why not?! The answer, I would suggest, is not simply that as rituals go this would be a pretty outlandish one. When my Dad was young people used to swing a chicken around their heads on the day before Yom Kippur so that it would absorb their sins from the previous year. And we ourselves every Rosh Hashanah go down by the riverside (or, more precisely, to the Chestnut Hill pond), heaving pieces of bread into the water, to symbolically carry away our sins and transgressions. Now what would an outsider, witnessing such behavior, say?

The answer is this, folks. A ritual, to be a ritual, must be repetitive. It must be engaged in on recurring occasions. And these occasions began, most meaningfully, not during our lifetime, but before, even long before, by our forebears, our ancestors, who imbued these occasions with significance through their performance of—stylized behavior. Yes, they had style! They didn't rush or slouch or slide through life. They inherited patterns of behavior, rituals of conduct, which had particular meanings like, *"This 'bread of affliction' is to remind you of how God rescued you from the abyss of slavery,"* but also an overall meaning like, *"Slow down. Life matters. Do something you share with others to take notice of the momentousness of human existence."*

Unlike many moderns, the "unsophisticated people" who preceded us were not marooned in the brief slice of time occupied by their individual lives. They felt connected to, rooted in, the past of their ancestors. And they had a teaching and a way with a significance for the future. This liberated them from the frantic, excessive need for individual distinction. This liberated them to participation in a cause which transcended and encompassed generations.

Life, at least in this world, is not everlasting. But everlasting significance may be felt here. We take up the Matzah on Pesach, remembering the liberation of our ancestors from Egypt, the House of Bondage. And through their liberation, we ourselves become the inheritors of freedom. Yet, with the Matzah we look forward, too, to the hoped-for redemption from all enslavement and injustice, embodied in the Messianic vision. We are united with the past and linked to the future. We are not dwellers on an island in time, disconnected from generations preceding and generations yet to come.

And so, participate in our ritual. Draw on this age-old way to invigorate your life in the present and open up vistas of hope and striving for the future. And then perhaps the day will come when you, too, feel adorned with a new spirit and new aliveness, one which comes wafting down like manna from— heaven.

"GIVEN THE BOOT"
An Episode from *The Adventures of a Hebrew School Rebel*

Here we were, American teenagers listening to our Hebrew high school teacher, Dov Parshan, as he discoursed on the nature of reality according to Kabbalah. It was rather amazing hearing a discussion of Jewish mysticism in those years at a Conservative synagogue in the Midwest, and probably out here in the East, as well. We were at Congregation Shaarey Zedek of Detroit, Michigan, a bastion of rational, sane Judaism, listening as our instructor, a Lubavitcher Hasid, tried to imbue us with mystical insight and illumination. When I say that our institutional approach was rational, I don't want to suggest that it was emotionless. It was not. But recourse to mystical speculation was hardly typical. I should add that the presence of a Lubavitcher teacher on a Conservative faculty was also atypical—for him, as well as for us.

Before accepting his appointment to the Shaarey Zedek faculty, Mr. Parshan had to receive permission from higher authorities in the Lubavitcher world. I might add that despite his religious proclivities, Mr. Parshan had an appearance distinctly un-Hasidic. He looked like any modern Orthodox male, meaning like any other American male, with a yarmulke, however, covering his head. Even his *peyot*, or ritual earlocks, were more like sideburns of moderate length. But the thought emerging from Mr. Parshan on the day in question was one which was bound to elicit a response, more precisely—a challenge.

As I mentioned, Mr. Parshan was attempting to instruct us in the Kabbalistic vision of the nature of reality. I later learned that what he told us, in fact, originated with the ancient Greeks and was the first Western effort at explaining the chemical make-up of the natural world. In those days, I should mention, the prevailing scientific view was that there were ninety-six elements. (Since that time approximately one-hundred-and-six have been asserted to exist.) Well, as Mr. Parshan put it, the world was composed of four elements, fire, water, earth and air. When I heard him say there were only four elements, I raised my hand and asked, "What happened to the other ninety-two?"

Mr. Parshan promptly booted me out of the class, angered by my insolence and heresy.

Now I should note that Mr. Parshan was, in fact, regarded with affection by my buddies and myself. While we didn't always agree with his religious outlook, we felt that he genuinely liked us and was sincere in his efforts to train—or transform—our "pagan" minds. But the reason I have chosen to dwell on him is because of the profounder truth which is contained in the Kabbalistic doctrine he valued. Interestingly, it is one with which we are addressed each year on Tu Bishvat, the Jewish New Year of Trees.

Obviously, this holiday encourages us to appreciate the beauties and wonders of nature. It encourages us to not take for granted the amazing world in which we live. But the Kabbalists of sixteenth century Safed, in the Land of Israel, developed a new consciousness and understanding regarding Tu Bishvat. For nature, they emphasized, is not simply the creation of God, but is a medium of His indwelling presence. It is an arena for His active participation in our lives. When we behold nature, we perceive only the outer garb. But behind the awe-inspiring appearance is a Spirit who animates, influences and pervades our very existence. Thus, felt the Kabbalists, Tu Bishvat should be a holiday when we attempt to heighten our awareness of the presence of God, who is, yes, beyond nature, as its Creator, but also within it, as its heart and soul. When we see a flower in bloom, when we behold the sun at dawn, when we are cooled by the waving branches of an overarching tree, we should feel that all these are intimations of a spiritual presence Who is attempting to restore us... to ourselves. The outer appearance is a sign of an inwardness, unseen yet real, who inhabits our world and wishes to reach us.

This emphasis on the inner, I believe, is the explanation for the abiding effectiveness of Jewish worship. Of course, we ask to be steered toward righteous action and moral deed. Of course, we pray for the wellbeing of the entire community of Israel, as for peace in the entire world. But a service succeeds in influencing an individual because of its impact on his or her soul. In the midst of the hurly-burly of life, we pause to raise our consciousness toward what really matters inside. Regardless of the honors we have or have not received, do we feel that we matter? Do our lives have a significance beyond the duration of our being here? Inside is there "quiet desperation" or inner repose?

In the homeyness of the weekday Minyan, as in the fellowship of sanctuary services, one may relax, feeling the support of others whose ultimate hopes and concerns are identical to one's own. Here one doesn't have to "prove oneself." One can simply be oneself, participating in a pause... that genuinely refreshes. Here one matters not for one's outer attainments, but simply because one is kin— spiritual kin, as we all are.

Woody Allen once got bounced out of a class not for challenging his teacher's Kabbalistic outlook, but because he cheated on an exam. As he says, it was a philosophy class, and his teacher caught him... looking into the soul of a neighbor! Well, I can assure you that if you come to our chapel and look into the soul of your neighbor, you will not feel you are an outsider, but rather that you are inside—in a fellowship formed from heart to heart.

Whether the world is formed out of four elements or ninety-six or one-hundred-and-six, inside there is one element, your inner self, which receives support, encouragement, friendship and reinforcement in a milieu which is founded on fellowship, on the community of the—MINYAN. The chapel, like the sanctuary, is the place. If you come, you may find out that you, too, are a closet... Kabbalist!

THE SOUNDS OF SILENCE

It was my final summer as a camper at Camp Ramah in Canada. As a teenager from Detroit, I spent my summers in the land to our north, thoroughly enjoying the climate, the program and the contact with friends from locales across a wide expanse.

This particular summer was especially memorable. For some reason the rambunctious group I belonged to was chosen to direct the camp's water day, which was a major event each summer.

The day went very successfully and that inspired us to embark on the preparation and performance of a play without much time remaining in the camp season. The play was "West Side Story," and I can still remember the emotional intensity of finally bringing it to fruition with only two days to go before we would return home.

Time has gone by and memories of that experience come back, as my daughter is now beginning to prepare for her own participation in that great musical by Leonard Bernstein. And we even have a similarity in roles, each belonging, in different casts, to the Puerto Rican gang, the Sharks.

"All right," you might be thinking. "How is Wolok going to link this little tale of drama and emotion to his professional focus, Jewish tradition and observance?" Well, I think there is a way. In "West Side Story" we see an intense identification with turf. The Sharks, like their rivals, the Jets, gain a sense of importance by being able to claim that a particular area is their own.

Now in the Jewish case, too, there is a link to place, though one that goes beyond the superficial claim to a location which just happens to be one's neighborhood. Analysts of human behavior have long understood that a positive sense of self is linked to one's identification with a place in which one truly has roots. Turf, in a deeper-than-accidental sense, is important. In fact, it is so important, that even if it is lost for a period of time, the "mere" memory of it may sustain and energize one through periods of suffering and exile.

If that place is, moreover, regarded as the geographical source and symbol of one's deepest values, then it is experienced as home in the richest way. Such is Jerusalem in the Jewish psyche, as we proclaim each time we read from the Torah scroll, "For from Zion shall come forth the Torah, and the Word of God from Jerusalem."

On Saturday evening, July 28, this year, beginning at 8:15 P.M., we will once again begin our observance of Tisha B'Av, the fast day on which we commemorate the destruction of the first and second temples in ancient Jerusalem, as well as other tragedies, such as the expulsion from Spain, which began on that very day. We will sing. We will recite. We will chant from the special Biblical text associated with Tisha B'Av, or *Eichah*, the Book of Lamentations, thereby reliving the pain and sorrow of ancient loss.

Even if the Jewish link to Jerusalem were not under present challenge, we would continue to find meaning in this special day. For we do not simply recall exile and suffering. Rather we gain strength from our frank confrontation with that which threatened our very existence, knowing that we persevered and that we shall persevere, now and in the future.

During that final summer I spent as a camper at Ramah I was privileged to hear Rabbi David Wolf Silverman, our scholar-in-residence, give a talk on Tisha B'Av evening. I remember some of what he said, but more significantly, the fact that when he finished, there was a silence in the room. Rabbi Silverman was quivering, and no one felt the impulse to speak.

More precisely, to speak at that moment seemed like a violation of a silence which was no mere absence of sound, but the felt presence of a holiness which transcended words. It was the holiness of Jewish sacrifice over the centuries, sacrifice for that which we identify with Jerusalem, a place which is much more than "mere turf."

I would like to invite you to participate in our Tisha B'Av service on July 28. If you would like to chant from *Eichah,* please let me know. If you do not yet know how to read from this text, I will gladly teach you. If you "simply" wish to attend, that, too, is of critical importance.

In gathering together we will experience not a mere claim to turf for one's own personal glory. We will experience a link to a location, which, unlike that of the Sharks and the Jets and many—or most— in the Palestinian community, does not deny the link which others feel. We will experience the hold upon us of the home from whence we as a people stem, from whence, no less, the message of universal justice and peace was first proclaimed.

Come to our Tisha B'Av service. God willing, we will there hear "sounds of silence" which are not empty, but resound with an eternal call both from our ancestors and from generations yet unborn.

LATKES FOR PESACH

If you came to my Baba Fannie's for a Passover Seder, you would not have to wait in order to eat. Before the telling of the story of the Exodus had even begun you would be greeted with—Latkes. Yes, Latkes! The special food for Chanukah, which occurs eight months later—or four months earlier, if you wish—would grace your palate, spinning the neurons of your brain into a state of confusion concerning season and celebration, tale and historical sequence.

Was it Antiochus who enslaved our ancestors in Egypt? And Mattathias who championed the cause of freedom in confrontation with the Egyptian ruler? Did the Jews leave Syria, home of the tyrannical Greeks, to cross the Sea of Galilee into the Land of Israel? And did Moses command the valiant Maccabees?

Now I don't want to suggest that while eating my grandmother's Latkes I was focusing primarily upon questions of chronology concerning our people's past. The taste and gastronomic delight of the present was pre-eminent in my experience. Still for a child, at least, my grandmother's custom could tend to lead to a merging of the lessons of Pesach and Chanukah, two holidays dedicated, in different ways, to the theme of freedom.

Pesach, as we know, is dedicated to remembering our people's dramatic liberation from bondage. Other peoples besides our own have seen in this tale a source of inspiration when plunged into the pit of slavery and oppression. But, it should be noted, the focus in the traditional recounting is not on our ancestors' efforts to break the chains which contained them, but rather on the irresistible and passionate will of God to free His people. Pesach is a holiday on which we recall and express gratitude for God's having helped us.

Now in the eyes of the rabbis Chanukah, too, commemorates an event in which God is the ultimate agent of change. Thus, in the "Al Hanisim" prayer recited at that time, we proclaim, "You delivered the mighty into the hands of the weak, and the many into the hands of the few." It was not our efforts, but God's, which determined the outcome of the struggle between those loyal to Judaism and those who would suppress it.

Still if God is the ultimate force enabling the victory of the Maccabees, it is also true that God was here helping those who helped themselves. Prayer alone did not avail. The unearned love and grace of God did not turn the day. Uncertain of victory, our ancestors stepped forth and initiated action on their own. If this, too, be seen as a response to an inner impulse from God, pushing us to the assertion of our own freedom and dignity and adherence to principle, then it is a response which still depends upon us.

You can lead a human being to the waters of salvation, but you cannot make him to drink. Our ancestors drank. And so, Chanukah is not simply the celebration of a victory. It is a holiday with a critical, pivotal notion, the partnership of God and humans, the affirmation of human effort and human assertiveness in the divine scheme of liberation.

Now if my grandmother's providing of Latkes on Pesach provoked thoughts about the themes of freedom and the divine-human relation, then I would have to say a more frequent association may be found between the "realm of food" and the "realm of spiritual reflection," and that is in the set of prayers recited after every meal, or the *Birkat HaMazon.* For the concluding line of this liturgical piece reads as follows, "The Lord will give strength unto His people; the Lord will bless His people with peace."

Peace is not simply a blessing which "plops down from heaven." Peace is a blessing which requires a recognition of the ability of the Jewish people to resist any threat to its existence. Human prowess is not to be feared. Only its reckless exercise it to be guarded against. We eat, and upon receiving nourishment, thank God for helping us to help ourselves.

When Theodor Herzl, the brilliant and charismatic leader of political Zionism, wanted to instill hope in his people, he wrote in his manifesto, *The Jewish State*, "The Maccabees shall rise again." Let us never forget the liberation from Egypt, undergone by slaves who could barely help themselves. But let us see in the story of Chanukah a further stage in the drama of redemption, and that is when people "take things into their own hands," not for selfish reasons, but in the service of higher ideals and eternal truths.

Thank you, Baba Fannie. From you I have learned the hidden message contained in that which may precede the Passover Seder. From you I have learned the spiritual teaching and exalted lesson of... LATKES FOR PESACH!

REVEALING REVELATION
The Case of the Junior Ritual Directors

Shortly we will be observing the festival of Shavuot, on which we rejoice over the revelation of the Torah. The words of this great text have received the attention of scholars and students for centuries— and even millennia. Multiple levels of meaning, hidden implications and nuances have been uncorked in the effort to encounter this text as both a fount of wisdom and a guide toward the righteous life.

It is interesting to note that in the eyes of the Torah there is a whole revelation which goes beyond the words of the Torah itself. Over and over again the Torah informs us that people are going about with their eyes closed, not only to the Torah, but to the world and to other people! Hagar, desperate with worry over her son, Ishmael, does not realize that right nearby is a well of water from which he can drink. And then we read that God opened her eyes.

The brothers of Joseph stare him in the face, but are not aware that it is their brother upon whom they look. Finally, his mask falls and a soul-to-soul meeting between the alienated siblings is facilitated. Blindness is not only physical. There is a paralysis of our consciousness, sometimes even a "hardening of our heart," which makes seeing difficult even though our eyes are intact.

In the prayer, "*Sim Shalom*," we speak of the Torah as a "*Torat Chayim*," a Torah of life. The purpose of the Torah is to put us in touch with the wonder of life and of the world in which we dwell. It is to tune us into the preciousness which is inscribed in every human face. It is to enable us to see the spiritual revelation which is here and now in our everyday world.

At our weekday services in Mishkan Tefila you will not always hear me, your ritual director, calling out the pages of the service. Frequently, young children, our "junior ritual directors" (and any child may become one), perform this task. I lean over and whisper into their ear the next page to be announced, and they in their endearing, spontaneous and enthusiastic way do the job.

If the world could truly hear the voices of children and experience the preciousness which sings forth from them, perhaps people would relinquish their enmity and turn toward each other in friendship and peace. Torah is not only a teaching. Torah is also life.

Come to Mishkan Tefila and experience a revelation which God is transmitting through the voices and hearts of our children. Then every day will be a mini-Shavuot and the word of the Lord which goes forth from Jerusalem will be a constant presence here in Chestnut Hill.

Section III

TRAINING FOR THE BIG TIME

*"Spring Training":
An Open Letter to You—If You're Twelve!
"Haftarah Brain Teasers"
"Maria, Maria"
"No Fat, No Cholesterol:
A Torah Diet for the Nineties"
"Deadly Serious"*

"SPRING TRAINING":
An Open Letter to You—If You're Twelve!

Dear Simchah:

I know you must be tired of people saying it. It seems just like yesterday you "showed up." Time flies and now, in one year's time, your entrance into the adult community of the Jewish people will be celebrated. You will become Bar or Bat Mitzvah.

I hope you don't mind, but for the purposes of this letter I have decided to give you my own personal nickname, Simchah. It seems to fit, because Simchah can be used for both a male and a female, and I really want to address both you and all your friends who will be "taking to the mound"—or ascending the bimah—during this coming year.

Simchah, furthermore, means a joyous occasion, a celebration, and that's what it will be when you "throw out your first pitch" as an adult member of the Jewish people. Everyone in the "stands"—or congregation—will be on your side. Everyone will be rooting for you—even those people whom you don't know personally.

If they're in *shul*, if they're in the synagogue, then they identify with Judaism and the Jewish people. How depressed they would be if you weren't there, joining the adult staff of our team that has been in existence for almost four thousand years, living a philosophy which both deserves and promises to go on for—eternity. And how happy they will be when you make your opening nod to the crowd.

You know, I must give credit where credit is due. Several weeks ago Cindy Yanofsky, a "coach" for one of our Mishkan Tefila families, came into my office and said you needed an inspirational message about this whole Bar and Bat Mitzvah thing. It's not just an empty ceremony. It's the advancement to a new level of maturity both in deciding how you will live and in living that way, with character, courage, compassion and a commitment to community as an ultimate value and concern. With Shavuot, the holiday celebrating the giving of the Torah, coming up at the end of the month, this seemed a good time to put out the message.

Now I don't mean to make everything sound heavy. And certainly

51

my childhood rabbi, Morris Adler, of blessed memory, didn't mean to when he cracked a joke at the first opportunity on my Bar Mitzvah day. I had just sat down beside him, when he pointed to the place where I would be standing when I chanted my Haftarah. He explained that there was a trapdoor there and if I made a mistake, he would push a button. Down I would go!

Now of course he was kidding. And I suppose it was a sign of confidence in me that he would venture such a joke. But the main thing is that mixed in with the seriousness of the moment there will also, God willing, be a joy and lightness of spirit that will contribute to your feeling of fulfillment. More than you may realize you are entering into a new phase of life, and excitement in response to your religious "rite of passage" will be natural. Here are some things to consider as you become a person wrestling with and entertaining new ideas and new thoughts.

Judaism is old, but the new world of today still needs it—badly. We are great with technology, but values like community and the absolute importance of every individual require strengthening. As a Jew all you need to do is step into a synagogue, literally anywhere in he world, and you are already part of a group. Our Torah, at the same time, teaches that every human being is unique and irreplaceable. Even where there are physical similarities, the feelings, the responses to the world, the vision, are individual. No person is a Xerox copy! Finally, living now you are not marooned in a brief slice of time. You are related to people going back millennia and carry a heritage for the future which will deepen your own sense of personal identity and worth.

I know I've spoken to a degree in generalities. But as that great American writer, Mark Twain, said, the Jewish people has outlasted countless empires that imagined they would rule the world. Amazingly, study has been one of the key ingredients in our survival. When the Romans defeated the Jewish state in the year 70, Rabbi Yochanan ben Zakkai asked if he could build an academy in Yavneh, in the Land of Israel, for the study of Torah. How out of touch Rabbi Yochanan must have seemed to the mighty Romans. But guess what. The Roman empire is gone and we are here!

With a commitment to Jewish learning you will feel your Jewish identity strengthened. And with that your respect for and love of our teachings and practices and outlook will grow and deepen. Our little people has inspired the world with its call to love one's neighbor as oneself, with its demand that nation shall not lift up sword against nation, with its vision of universal respect, of social justice and of individual character. In addition, we enrich ourselves through our own ritual observance, both at home and in the synagogue, by creating a sense of the specialness of life and of the presence of God when we are together.

Soon "spring training" will be over and you will "take to the field, ascending the mound for your first pitch." On that day, when you make your commitment to Judaism and the Jewish people, you will put your own special "spin on the ball." For singing and speaking are more than hitting the notes and reciting the words. Your own soul and personality will come through, and to that we say, "Right on!"

And so, dear Simchah, it is with Simchah that we welcome you into the adult community of People Israel. Your participation on our team is looked forward to, as it is deeply valued and cherished.

Sincerely,
Dr. Davin Wolok

HAFTARAH BRAIN TEASERS

Some time ago the policy was instituted of having our Bar and Bat Mitzvahs not only chant their Haftarahs, but give introductions to them. While brief in duration, the introductions serve as an important means of enabling the congregation to appreciate the significance of the Biblical texts to come. Of course, the study and effort invested in the preparation of the Haftarah introductions enlighten the students as to the meaningfulness and depth of the material they have learned.

As a way of suggesting how challenging and intriguing the Haftarahs are, I will present a series of questions which arise when reflecting upon a number of them. I call them "Haftarah Brain Teasers." Hopefully, as you listen to our students speak, you will be further attuned to the richness of the material with which we, as Jews, have our young people deal in their rite of passage as adolescents. May their insights both enlighten you and increase your own interest in our sacred texts.

And now for the "brain teasers."

In a Haftarah associated with the Parshah (weekly Torah portion) of Shemot, God says to the prophet, Jeremiah, that He had a personal knowledge of him even before he was formed in his mother's womb. How is that possible? What can that possibly mean?

In the same Haftarah God recalls how the Jewish people loyally followed Him in the Wilderness of Sinai, after the time of the Exodus from Egypt. The Torah repeatedly states that the opposite occurred. Why this contradiction between the Haftarah and the words of the Torah?

In the Haftarah associated with the Parshah of Tzav God states that He did not command the giving of sacrifices when the Jews were in the wilderness. Again, the Torah states the opposite. How are the words of this Haftarah to be understood? Literally? Non-literally? If the latter, why? And what could be the non-literal meaning?

In the Haftarah associated with the Parshah of Bamidbar God speaks of the Jewish people as His wife. The Hebrew word for husband, it should be noted, is "*baal*," which means lord or master. The word for wife is "*ishah*," which also means simply woman. God

54

states that He looks forward to the day when the Jewish people no longer call Him "my *baal*," but rather "my *ish*." "*Ish*" currently means only man, but God wants it to mean husband, as well, just as "*ishah*" means both woman and wife. What might this promised linguistic change imply about the ideal nature of a relationship when the partners are not God and a people, but two human beings?

In the Haftarah associated with the Parshah of Behar the prophet, Jeremiah, purchases a plot of land, even though he has already proclaimed that due to the sins of the people, Israel shall be conquered by the Babylonians. Why would anyone in his right mind engage in a purchase of real estate, when he believes that shortly after doing so he will lose it? Was Jeremiah bonkers... or brilliant? Whatever you say, say why!

I hope you have enjoyed the above "Haftarah Brain Teasers." May you be enriched by the words of our students on the day that they pass into Jewish religious maturity.

"MARIA, MARIA"

Did you ever think you would come to the synagogue and hear the music of Leonard Bernstein's "West Side Story?" I don't mean during the performance of a musical. I mean during a Shabbat morning service. In fact, you will. If you listen closely to our students chanting the words, "Adonai, Eloheinu," in the blessing preceding a Haftarah, you will note that the music is identical to that of Tony, the male lead in Bernstein's musical, when he sings out the name of his beloved, "Maria, Maria."

As is well known, Bernstein was himself Bar Mitzvah at Mishkan Tefila, and it is entirely possible that the music he learned for that occasion made its way into "West Side Story." In an ongoing effort to bring humor and human interest into my Bar and Bat Mitzvah tutoring I point out to the students the above surprising relationship between a great American musical and the music of their "big day." Of course, I remind them to sing the words of the Hebrew prayer and not "Maria, Maria" while chanting their Haftarah blessing. And perhaps this unnecessary warning itself adds a touch of fun to our lessons together.

While normally I report on new developments—or ongoing issues—in our synagogue ritual life, I thought an "insight" into our students' learning would be a source of interest and delight to you, as well.

So, come to our Shabbat morning services. What you believe you are hearing while there might not only be in your imagination!

"NO FAT, NO CHOLESTEROL"
A Torah Diet for the Nineties

"Taste and see that the Lord is good." So instructs us the author of the Book of Psalms. Beginning this year the Vav class in the religious school is partaking of a Torah diet, with many new flavors added to an already rich menu.

When one looks into a text of the Torah one notices, in addition to the words themselves, symbols which show how the text is to be sung. These symbols are called "Trop" or "Taamei HaMikrah." Outwardly, these symbols are identical to those which guide the singing of Haftarahs and other selections from the Bible. But what we sing when we see these symbols varies from one part of the Bible to the next.

In the past the emphasis in the religious school has been on learning how the symbols or trop are sung when one is chanting a Haftarah. This skill will continue to be an important component of the students' learning, beginning with the Hey class. But this year the Vav class will learn how to sing the trop when chanting a portion of the Torah.

Interestingly, the other term for trop, "Taamei HaMikrah," or "The Cantillations of Scriptures," may be poetically understood as "The Flavors of Scripture." Thus, in learning the Torah trop the students are, in effect, learning "The Flavors of Torah." Perhaps there is the suggestion that in addition to what the mouth can taste there is food which the soul can savor. And such "soul food" is totally lacking in unhealthy ingredients. Sing this "fat-free, cholesterol-free" Torah diet and your weight will go down through the calories expended in the singing!

We hope that the Vav students not only master a skill for their Bar or Bat Mitzvahs—and beyond!— but that they experience the Torah, through music, as rich, flavorful and permanently appealing. Perhaps in an age of fast food there is a place for that which not only nourishes, but lasts.

DEADLY SERIOUS

I would like you to consider the following passages and figure out what they have in common. Here's the first one: "Larry threw the basketball. Kevin caught the ball and threw it into the basket."

Number two: "A heavy proton was wearing pants. A friendly atom went riding on a bicycle and came quickly over to the house of his brother, Maximillian, a charming atom."

Number three: "Rivka, a good woman from Boston, the major city in the state, bought a VCR to see videos. She ate Cheerios during the videos. She also put on the CD of an excellent singer, and ate more cheerios while listening to the CD."

And finally: "Moses ate pizza."

Do you see the connection? Isn't it obvious? All of the above quotations are trop exercises!

Trop?... What's that???

Trop are the musical symbols which are put above or below the words of a Biblical text, for example, a Torah reading or a Haftarah. They tell the one doing the chanting how to sing the words so as to convey the meaning of the text.

Each week I come into the Hey and Vav classes of our religious school to teach the students the basics which they will need to know for their Bat or Bar Mitzvahs. Central among these is the ability to sing the trop, so that they will be more ready when they are engaged in individualized preparation for their "big day."

It is, of course, easy for the learning of any skill requiring practice and repetition to become a "rendezvous with boredom." So as to introduce an element of fun into the effort to master the trop, I created (or perhaps more accurately, concocted) the above "texts," to which I applied the trop. These texts, in addition to Biblical texts, are sung by the students while they are in the learning period. Hopefully, when a knowledge of the trop has been attained, a feeling of pleasure will remain and become attached to the process of mastering a Haftarah or Torah portion.

Two quotations come to mind as I consider the trop exercises. The first is from King David, who wrote, "Serve the Lord with joy."

The second is from a great philosopher, who proclaimed, "Nothing human is alien to me." May our Hey and Vav students realize that basketball, atomic science, high tech and pizza all have a role to play in their knowing participation in a culture which will both energize and uplift them.

And now... please pass the oregano!

Section IV

FROM THE LITTLE RED SCHOOLHOUSE
TO LIFE IN OUTER SPACE

"Synagogue Chanting Skills as Taught in a Little Red Schoolhouse"
"An Anthropologist on Mars"
"Ritual Minis:
The Bite Size Approach to Observance"
"Rebellion, Passion, Guts and Redemption:
Hollywood? No, the Bible!"
"Where Art Thou?": Biblical Reflections in an Age of Madness,
Materialism and the Quest for Meaning
"The Wild West and Capital City"
"Jewish Thought in an Age of Coca Cola and the Computer"
"Blast Off!:
A Journey into the Outer Reaches of Inner Space"
"The Right Door: An Adventure for Spiritual Explorers"
"A Conversation between Lovers:
The Bible as Testimony to a Tumultuous Marriage"
"Oedipus Shmoedipus"

SYNAGOGUE CHANTING SKILLS
AS TAUGHT IN A LITTLE RED SCHOOLHOUSE

A great modern philosopher, Ludwig Wittgenstein, wrote, "To pray is to think about the meaning of life." In this course you will learn how to pray and hopefully to think more fully—and feelingly—about the meaning of your life.

Do you want to learn the chanting of the daily services? Do you want to read Torah? With the direct, engaged approach of a teacher in a "little red schoolhouse" the ritual director—yours truly—will attempt to provide students with the skills to lead daily *davening* (praying) and/or read Torah, so that hopefully, as a result, we will sense more fully the meaningfulness of our lives as Jews and as Jewish worshippers.

In addition to instruction in the music of our services, discussion will focus on both "oddities" and issues of wider scope in our liturgy. Why, for example, does the acrostic psalm, "*Ashrei*," lack a line for the letter, "nun?" Did the author just slip up? Or was there an intention behind the "oversight?" How can the second paragraph of the "*Shema*," not easily accepted literally, be understood as forecasting the current ecological crisis? How may "hoary tradition" in synagogue music in fact be the product of a revolutionary spirit?

The study in our "little red schoolhouse" will appeal with music to your heart and with concept to your mind. And if we should add the traditional *shuckling*, or swaying to and fro while praying, to our learning, the course may even enhance your physical fitness!

Come to our "little red schoolhouse" and join in a multi-faceted educational experience meant to lift you up to God and enable you to taste the "meaning of life."

AN ANTHROPOLOGIST ON MARS

It was my good fortune this Chanukah to receive as a gift *An Anthropologist on Mars*, a book by the British-American neurologist, Oliver Sacks. Author of another well-received work, *The Man Who Mistook His Wife for a Hat*, Sacks in his newer work describes the efforts, usually successful, of individuals suffering neurological damage to cope with their daunting conditions.

The title of the book derives from the self-description of an autistic college professor, reflecting her experience of the emotional dimension of human relations as somewhat mysterious and impenetrable.

What caught my attention in reading Sacks' book was the positive role played by music in providing individuals suffering from major neurological conditions with a sense of peace and equanimity. That it could bring serenity to a person suffering from Tourette's Syndrome was quite striking. That he functioned as a surgeon was even more amazing.

It has long been known that music exerts a profound emotional impact on people of all cultural backgrounds. Not infrequently figures of distinction in the world of the intellect have acknowledged that music transcends, in what it conveys, the realm of concepts in which they specialize. Music stirs. Music uplifts. Music brings peace.

Happily, increasing numbers of our Mishkan Tefila members have become involved in the musical life of our congregation. Whether reading Torah, chanting a Haftarah or intoning the plaintive strains of *The Book of Lamentations* on Tisha B'Av, congregants have participated to an enlarged degree in our religious services.

Continuing to study the traditional musical modes of our daily services, a number of congregants have also mastered and sung the prayers of the special Hallel service, recited on festivals and at the beginning of a new month in the Jewish calendar.

I would like to take this opportunity to renew my invitation to all Mishkan Tefila members to learn the musical modes of both Bible and prayerbook. Let us not be strangers to this powerful medium of our tradition. Let us, who are not called upon to demonstrate the heroic efforts of an *anthropologist on Mars*, acquire an at-homeness with our music, which is all so readily available to us.

The door is open.

Welcome home.

RITUAL MINIS
A Bite Size Approach to Observance

In my adult education teaching at Mishkan Tefila I have tried to offer courses focused on both the intellectual and practical dimensions of Judaism. As discussed in last month's bulletin, my course this year in the former category will be an examination of life issues (e.g. family relations, personal independence, the call to higher service) as presented in the Bible. Utilizing a traditional mode of Jewish expression, namely, the question, it is called, "'WHERE ART THOU?': Biblical Reflections in an Age of Madness, Materialism and the Quest for Meaning."

In the latter category, the practical, I am once again offering a course entitled, "SYNAGOGUE CHANTING SKILLS AS TAUGHT IN A LITTLE RED SCHOOLHOUSE." In reality it is a series of specialized courses in which I teach congregants, on an individualized basis, the chanting of daily services, Torah reading and other musical components of our religious services. Scheduling for such courses is done in consultation with interested congregants.

This year I would like to add a new element in my adult education teaching. It, too, will take place on an individualized basis, or if a number of congregants have a common interest and can meet at the same time, will involve a group dimension. This is a course entitled, "RITUAL MINIS: A Bite Size Approach to Observance." There are congregants who would like to master some of the specific components of our religious observance, without necessarily learning how to lead an entire portion of a service. Such congregants may, for example, want to know how to chant the Friday evening Kiddush, or prayer over wine, so as to enhance their experience of the Shabbat. The very beautiful Havdalah ceremony, concluding the Shabbat, may also become an element of home observance and can be studied in the context of "RITUAL MINIS." How to shake the Lulav and Etrog while reciting a blessing or during the Hallel service on Sukkot, how to put on Tefillin (which can also be taught in the chapel right before a weekday morning service) and, in fact, any other element of our ritual life can be learned within this "Bite Size Approach to Observance." The choice is yours.

The great Jewish thinker, Abraham Joshua Heschel, spoke of the music of the Mitzvot, that element of upliftment experienced in the practice of the ritual which goes beyond all of the explanations as to the rituals' particular meanings. On the High Holidays (and not only then) we must be verbally reminded of the need for repentance. But the message of the words is enhanced when we hear the blasts of the Shofar. On Pesach we eat Matzah not only to call to mind the Exodus from Egypt, but to connect, in a physical-emotional way, with our ancestors and feel "in our bones" the earth-shattering importance of freedom. On Simchat Torah we dance to palpably experience, and not merely meditate on, the way in which Torah may transport us to a higher plane.

Jewish observance needn't be "gobbled down" all at once. It can be learned in a "bite size" manner and both slowly and meaningfully integrated into one's life. Similarly, you don't have to come to a chapel service every week in order to experience the fulfillment which comes from participation in "the Minyan." Attendance on the Yahrzeit, or anniversary of the death of a loved one, is a significant Mitzvah and an exquisite means of tasting the richness of our daily religious life. Becoming a regular, attending one or more services a week, may come to seem not a burden, but a means of fulfillment you wouldn't want to forego.

You have a range of opportunities for learning and participating in Jewish religious life. Begin, if you wish, with the "bite size" approach.

There is much on the menu. You may start with whichever course you prefer.

REBELLION, PASSION, GUTS AND REDEMPTION"
HOLLYWOOD? NO. THE BIBLE!

You think you have problems with your kids? What about David, top honcho in ancient Israel, whose son, Absalom, tried to overthrow him? What about Terach, successful businessman in Ur, whose son, Abraham, demolished his sculptures, leaving only "archeological remains?" What about God, Creator of the Universe, who made the human race, only to find it relishing in rebellion? And yes, God, does He have a simple role in all this? Is He not a fomenter of rebellion, Abraham against Terach, Moses against Pharaoh, Jonathan against Saul?

Family values, you say, that's what we need. Well, then should we be celebrating a man who cheats on his wife and arranges for the death of his loyal employee? No, I don't mean Absalom. I mean his papa, David, who was not, shall we say, the perfect role model. And the woman with whom he took up, Bathsheba... did she bathe in a location visible from the king's window because she *didn't* want to attract his attention? Was *au naturelle* just an accident? And again, God who proclaims his love for the People of Israel, doesn't He seem a bit like a burnt lover, raging when they are unfaithful to Him?

Guts, you want? Well, what about Deborah, a brave woman at a time when Israel was without central government, rallying the people in their battle against the powerful Canaanites? What about Samuel, who "read the riot act" to Saul, king of Israel, when he, the king, did not follow orders properly? What about Jeremiah who lambasted the Israelites for their wrongs and raised the murderous ire (thankfully not realized) of a number of his fellow citizens, including some of his relatives?

Is there any relief from this tale of intense emotion and momentous deed? Better, are there moments of redemption, times when hope for the good is realized and relationships, both with humans and with God, reach fulfillment? Does Jonathan ever walk with David? Does the one who descends to the "valley of the shadow of death" find himself not alone, but with God?

This year I will be offering a course entitled, "Rebellion, Passion, Guts and Redemption: The Bible As It Was—And Is." The class will meet on Wednesday evenings, beginning on October 13, at 7:20 P.M., following the evening Minyan. You are all cordially invited.

"WHERE ART THOU?"
Biblical Reflections in an Age of Madness, Materialism and the Quest for Meaning

When looking for Adam in the Garden of Eden, God asks, "Where art thou?" How surprising. Should not a being of supreme intelligence know where one of His creatures is hiding? Perhaps the question was not asked because God was seeking information. Perhaps the question was asked so that Adam would stop and heartfully reflect on where he had gotten to in life and in his relation to God.

As the German-Jewish philosopher, Franz Rosenzweig, noted, God's question to Adam is, in fact, addressed to every human being. Where are we? Successful more than ever before in satisfying our material needs, do we strive for a higher fulfillment? More importantly, do we strive to make fulfillment, even higher self-fulfillment, not our ultimate goal, but only a byproduct of serving goals transcending the self?

On Wednesday evening, beginning on October 21, following the evening Minyan, I will be giving a course entitled, "'WHERE ART THOU?': Biblical Reflections in an Age of Madness, Materialism and the Quest for Meaning." This will not be a course in philosophy, in which we, for example, attempt to prove the existence of God. Nor will it be a course in which we simply strive to understand or explain a diverse and wide-ranging set of Biblical texts. Rather we shall make an effort to be open to the Bible in the way in which it is attempting to address us. We shall study Biblical narrative, law, poetry and prophecy with the aim of understanding ourselves and our lives better.

As moderns we might, with Freud, think of a Greek figure, Oedipus, in trying to understand the human self. But who has not, at times, found himself or herself alone like Jacob, our ancestor, confronting a crisis and wrestling with the twin issues of higher duty and a concern for one's own well-being? Who has not, at times, like Jonathan, David's soul-brother, struggled with the intertwined themes of family ties, friendship and personal independence? Who has not like Esther strived to reconcile and/or been forced to choose between participation in the larger culture and loyalty to the group from which one comes? And to whom does God not say, "Where art thou?"

When our neuroses have been cured and our pockets are not empty, when we "have it all" and our loved ones do not lack, is there a voice calling us and summoning us to a life of duty, holiness and meaning? In an age in which we pride ourselves on our capacities as scientific-rational beings, yet bear witness—repeatedly—to massacre and mass murder, is there a basis for hope and the confidence that we matter, as individuals matter? Does the Bible matter?

Together we shall wrestle with this question and attempt to hear a voice which even in our time is hopefully not inaudible.

"WHERE ART THOU?"

THE WILD WEST AND CAPITAL CITY

Moses had just died, and the people were in a blue funk. They had no sense of stability anywhere in their lives. For unlike their parents who had left Egypt, even if as slaves, they had no experience of an established society, with institutions going back to times of yore. Only two of the earlier generation, Joshua and Caleb, remained to go with them into the Land of Canaan, as they alone had shown courage and hope and determination concerning the Jewish cause.

And then Joshua, the newly appointed leader, stepped forth. As with his mentor, Moses, the waters parted for him, too, but this time it was the waters of River Jordan, and the people passed through. On the edge of the ancient city of Jericho, an angel appeared to Joshua and commanded him, like Moses at the burning bush, to remove his shoes, for he was on holy ground. The restless band of exiles, neither enslaved nor yet at home, these "cowboys," if you will, had found their hero and guide, a man whose very name sends the message, "God shall save."

Beginning on Wednesday evening, October 25, at 7:20 P.M. in the library, following the Minyan, I will be offering a course entitled, "THE WILD WEST AND CAPITAL CITY: The Bible from 'Joshua Fought the Battle of Jericho' to King David is Alive and Well in Jerusalem." In it we will learn about how Joshua's people, with their "boom boxes," or "trumpets," as the Bible calls them, brought down the walls of mighty Jericho. We will learn about the tumultuous period following Joshua's death, when there was no central government for the Jewish people, and magnetic personalities, called "Judges" or "Chieftains," arose to save the people in the face of crisis or emergency. We will learn about individuals who are both admirable and troubling, inspiring and vexing, uplifting and perplexing.

Here is Samson, who had the strength of a professional wrestler prowling the ring, and the weakness of a male with an attraction to short skirts. Here is Deborah, who rallied the boys in their fight with Sisera, spurring on Barak (no, not Ehud), who directed them in battle. Here is Samuel, both a fighter against the Amalekites and a prophet calling out for obedience to God.

71

Then came the kings, first Saul, a he-man and victim of a bipolar disorder, who unified the people politically. And then came the individual who will be the central focus of our course, that richest of personalities from this period—David. Pre-eminent king of Israel, he established Jerusalem as its capital city and became, according to tradition, the forerunner of the Messiah himself. The limited material concerning him which was delved into last year will be briefly reviewed, as we explore the character and conflicts, the failures and triumphs, of an individual whose family life was tumultuous and whose political life was explosive in impact.

Not only an individual of strength and shrewdness, David was in his youth a music therapist and in adulthood, a poet. He is regarded as having crafted many of the Psalms, which we shall also explore in an effort to deal with our own struggles and emotions. Is God with us? Is there a light when darkness and danger abound? Are we on our own or not alone in our quest for meaning and stability and peace? In facing loss we call out, with David, "The Lord is my shepherd." When feeling torn apart, we turn to God, "The Healer of Broken Hearts." When challenged or threatened, we proclaim with our poet-king, "I shall not fear." The inner life, religious experience, psalm-and-prayer-and-meditation shall be the complementary dimension of our course, which also examines action-packed narrative. In addition to an intellectual exploration of text, we shall become acquainted with music for the Psalms, so that we might learn with our hearts, as well as our minds.

So, put on your cowboy hats and gallop in. It's Wednesday, October 25, at 7:20 P.M. that we'll begin. (Boom boxes are allowed.)

JEWISH THOUGHT IN AN AGE OF COCA COLA AND THE COMPUTER

The modern age is characterized, in large measure, by the pursuit of pleasure and the desire to achieve, through the expansion of knowledge, a mastery of the natural and human environment. While Judaism affirms the legitimacy of pleasure and power as elements in human life, it, more importantly, directs us toward the ultimate questions of existence, questions which can be avoided, but never totally escaped.

Are we alone in the universe or is there a higher reality who imbues our lives with meaning? Are we on our own in determining how to act and conduct ourselves or is there guidance which comes from a spiritual plane? Is the Jewish people the bearer of an ultimate purpose or is our existence a mere accident of history?

Challenging the exclusive importance of pleasure ("Coca Cola") and power-through-knowledge ("the Computer"), we will probe the views of Jewish thinkers on the intertwined themes of God, Torah and Israel, both to expand our intellectual understanding and to deepen our spiritual sensitivity.

Soft drinks and laptops will be permitted... for those who absolutely insist.

BLAST OFF!
A Journey into the Outer Reaches of Inner Space

I was attending my graduate seminar on "Philosophy and Technology" when a guest speaker appeared who had worked for NASA. He was going to speak on colonies the United States was planning to establish in outer space. At one point during his presentation he began to discuss the issue of farming and consumption, and I piped up, "Will there be kosher food?"

A fellow sitting in front of me apparently thought that keeping kosher was the special preserve of a particular Jewish movement, because he turned around and began to say, "But the Hassidim..." At which, I shot back, "Oh no, they don't need these gadgets to go into outer space!"

A Havurah, or fellowship group, is now under way, which you are invited to join, called, "Space Cadets: A Havurah for Spiritual Explorers." In it we are not learning how to be Hassidim, but we are trying to explore the outer reaches of inner space, the sphere we all feel, but don't always talk about, much less focus upon.

Our sessions, open to both couples and singles, involve, in varying combinations, music, ritual, study, reflection and meditation. What is the power in music such that, with or without words, it is capable of calming or uplifting us, dispelling depression and instilling hope? Our approach will be experiential, tasting first-hand Jewish music whose overt goal is to touch the soul.

What is the power in ritual such that it deepens our sense of meaning, even when we can't fully put that meaning into words? We will draw upon traditional and modern sources so as to ritually enrich our own sessions through food and text and emotionally evocative "atmospheric" elements. The inner meaning of outer symbols will be a topic of discussion.

What is the soul? Is there something in us which goes beyond our physical body? And if so, can paying attention to it enrich us both as individuals and in our interpersonal relationships, "Platonic" and otherwise? Is death the end? Is the Jewish talk of immortality and resurrection hooey? Contemporary reports of nonordinary, for example, near-death experiences, will combine with ideas both from Kabbalah and non-mystical Jewish sources to enliven our discussions.

Suggestive tales, as well as more "straight-talking" texts, will be a focus of attention. Expeditions outside our "space capsule," for example, to concerts or movies or plays related to our interest are a possibility, upon which the members may decide. Shabbat or holiday meals together are another option.

In essence, we will be in search of our—essence. What are we really, as human beings, as Jews, as a people? Do we have a spiritual nature, a purpose, a destiny which imbues our everyday duties and roles with meaning and holiness? Do we matter—eternally?

Please call the synagogue to learn details about meeting times and places for our Havurah. Without gadgets we will soar into inner space!

THE RIGHT DOOR
An Adventure for Spiritual Explorers

I can't remember her name. She was going with my friend from Borders Bookshop in Ann Arbor, having moved there from a town in Ohio. Over dinner one night she told a story about an unusual experience she had in her former town.

During a period of great stress, she went out walking one evening, only to discover that she had suddenly fallen into a state of amnesia. She had no idea who she was, yet miraculously was able to keep her wits about her.

First, she went to one house and was about to ring the doorbell to ask for help. But then a feeling overcame her that this was not the right place. So, she turned and headed across the street to another house, where she rang the doorbell, to be greeted by the woman who lived there.

The woman invited her in and listened to her story, after which she said, "This is very unusual. I never answer the door for strangers. But when you rang, I felt that I was supposed to answer. Now let me tell you. You have come to the right place. My husband will be home in a half-hour and he will find you help. He is the director of community mental health in this area."

The great American writer, Saul Bellow, believed that spiritual experience is widespread. Yet, we are often embarrassed to talk about anything that doesn't fit into a "scientific" view of things. Our prophets and sages presented the Torah as the revelation of God. Is this so? Or is it, as modern people are inclined to say, just the product of great human minds, "philosophers," if you will, who came up with notions like monotheism and the brotherhood-sisterhood of all people? Did God speak to Abraham and Moses and Isaiah, or did they "concoct" Judaism on their own?

Beginning on Wednesday, October 17, at 7:30 P.M., I will give a course entitled, "Prophets, Madmen or Philosophers?: The Vision of Judaism through Biblical Tale and Teaching." We will explore primarily narrative, but also legal, selections from the Torah, supplemented by later prophetic texts, clarifying the basic concepts of Judaism up to the present day.

God, creation, revelation, chosen peoplehood, Messianic redemption, ritual, ethics, suffering, faith, life after death, will be central concerns of our course. Challenging conventional beliefs, we will ask why Darwin affirmed that God was the author of the laws of nature. We will ask why the atheist, Nietzsche (author of the statement, "God is dead"), said that he experienced revelation. We will ask why neuroscientist, John Eccles, believed in life after death.

We will study the Bible so as to hopefully crack open our Jewish soul. In doing so, I believe, we will be knocking on the "right door." Please come in.

A CONVERSATION BETWEEN LOVERS
The Bible as Testimony to a Tumultuous Marriage

W e have been on a journey. We cannot say, from our own experience, when it began. Or at least we have no clear memory, though others tell us they can pinpoint the moment. First, we were in one realm and then suddenly in another. From the outside people could see when we emerged and began our travels. But for us, the ones experiencing and living the journey, there is no recollection of the beginning, much less of the realm before. We were involved in the journey before we had any clear idea of what was going on. We were in the middle of a stream before we even knew we were in a stream!

What am I referring to with the above analogy? What stream is this we were—or are — in the middle of, where looking back is not only an occasion for nostalgia or regret, but a means of rooting ourselves as we advance creatively in the future? My analogy is, of course, to life, to the lives we lead, each of us an individual venturing into existence without any preparatory lessons or practice session. From the womb of our mother we each emerged into a drama with no straight path, where there is both novelty and surprise, anticipation and reversal, disappointment and hope restored—without the sequence being predictable in advance.

And in the midst of this drama, this journey, we seek fulfillment as the individuals we are, discovering it principally through our relations with others, though not only human others. For in the eyes of our tradition, beginning with its foundational work, the Bible, we seek fulfillment also through a relation to our ultimate source of existence and meaning, or God. A duality pervades our relations at all levels.

In relation to our human fellows we seek to assert ourselves, yet at times feel challenged and thrown back. We strive for relations of depth, of friendship and love, yet are susceptible to envy and feelings of alienation. Jealousy and empathy may, indeed, jostle each other within a single heart. And in relation to God, too, we manifest conflicting sensibilities. We are lifted by awe, but feel tested by the presence of inscrutable evil. We show a dedication to the highest, the truly divine, ideals. And we worship our own ego.

This amazing mix of emotions, of impulses, of tendencies and temptations, is, I believe, the underlying reality, the living current, beneath the words of Holy Scripture. And this work of unsurpassable vitality and importance attempts to see the universal struggle of humanity through the prism of the relationship of one people and God, the People of Israel and their Creator who set them free.

Poignantly suggesting the powerful emotions present within this relationship, the Bible conceives of it as a relationship of marriage. God is a Mate and not only a Master. With love He attempts to bring Israel close to Him. Yet, He can feel burnt, as when He wants to divorce the Jewish people during the episode of the golden calf. Israel can be disloyal, running after false suitors, the pagan gods, the idols, which it at times cozies up to rather than sticking with the One whose care for her is genuine. Still when He looks back, He remembers the moments they were close, even in times of adversity.

This year I will be offering an adult education course which views the Bible as the result of the passionate, emotion-laden interaction between the Jewish People and God. In saying this, I am not speaking only of an ancient relationship. The Bible, I believe, is about us, with our emotions and our struggles and our conflicts and our hopes. With a recognition of the centrality of love not only in human-human relation and aspiration, but also in the human-divine—and Jewish-divine—relationship, I shall call the course, "A Conversation between Lovers: The Bible as Testimony to a Tumultuous Marriage." We shall commence our exploration of the Biblical text with our ancestors encamped at Mt. Sinai, awaiting God's revelation. The "scene at Sinai," the Ten Commandments and the immediate aftermath in betrayal and rebellion shall introduce us to the emotionally charged and rocky beginning of a relationship whose spiritual import reverberates to this day. The starting date for the course is Wednesday, October 9, at 7:30 P.M., following the evening Minyan. Look for the sign by the coat room saying, "Lovers rendezvous in the library—Bible study with passion!"

OEDIPUS SHMOEDIPUS

It took place in the eighties, while I was teaching at the Hebrew College. A friend on the faculty was short on cash and asked me if I could loan him some. "Of course," I said, thinking that was that. But he wanted to do something for me immediately and responded, "What can I do for you now?" I said, "Tell me two stories!" I meant stories from life, stories from his own life. There's something about stories I love, some way that these vignettes of life go beyond all the theories of psychologists and sociologists and physical scientists and philosophers in showing us who we are, in clueing us in to what truly makes us tick.

The psychologist may say, "It's an Oedipus complex," as if some general formula of psychological functioning could really grasp all the dimensions of an individual's life. The sociologist may tell us that we are as we are because of our economic class, as if a person could never think anything beyond what others in his class are inclined to. A physical scientist may say that we are simply the result of the atoms buzzing around in our brain, as if our thoughts and feelings were nothing more than the "steam" emitted by a "teakettle" formed of gray matter. A philosopher may view us as representatives of abstract principles, as if concrete people could be summed up as pure idealists or pure materialists and nothing more, nothing more complicated and interesting.

But a story, a "mere" story grabs us in a way that none of these theoretical approaches do. A story seizes us in our *kishkes* both because it is a slice of life and because down-deep we feel a kinship to what is going on. It does not matter if we have been in exactly the same situations or engaged in precisely the same actions. We have felt the same feelings. We have wrestled with the same issues. You don't have to throw your brother in a pit, as did Joseph's brothers, in order to experience sibling rivalry. And you don't have to start a revolution, as did Absalom, David's son, in order to resent being at the bottom of the generational heap.

Between all human souls there is a deep kinship. We are each a unique way of grappling with universal issues. The richness of a story, a truly great story, is that wherever we come from we can find ourselves in it. Freedom, love, mortality, faith, frustration, hope, redemption, these are the issues we encounter in truly great stories, reflections of our own experience in the unpredictable adventure known as human life.

Last month I wrote that my Bible course next year will be called, "Three Thousand Comments on Three Verses," because of my hope and expectation that people will express themselves to the fullest concerning the texts (more than three verses!) which we shall explore. This will not be an opportunity to just "spill our guts." Rather we shall encounter the Bible as itself a kind of "spiritual dynamite" exciting our reflection upon our ancestors, but no less upon—ourselves. The people of the past are not locked in the past. They are our kin, and through them we shall encounter both our neighbors and the people we see when we look into the mirror.

So, let me be specific. For one of my students asked, "But what texts are we going to focus on in our investigation into the Bible?" My answer brings me back to my colleague at the Hebrew College and the response I gave to his wish to give. It's stories, friends. It's stories that will concern us, beginning with the moment our ancestors pack up their tents and venture out from Sinai. Two tablets in their possession, they have only faith in God's presence to carry them, trembling into the future.

Do we have the courage? Do we have the courage to join them in a journey through a wilderness laden with both possibility and uncertainty, hope and the unexpected?

In exploring the stories of their trials and challenges, we will gain strength for the tests which face us, as well.

Section V

BALONEY IN THE GREAT BEYOND

"My Uncle Henry"
"A Rocking Celebration at the Mish"
"A Baloney Sandwich in Heaven"
"Football and Faith:
A Life with Lions and Tigers"
"Uncle Simcha"

MY UNCLE HENRY

There is hardly an American alive who has not seen "The Wizard of Oz" multiple times. We all recall Dorothy, her dog Toto and her wonderful Auntie Em. Interestingly, when I checked, few remembered that Dorothy also had an uncle, and so it goes without saying that they did not remember his name. "Uncle Henry," he was called, and while he played "second fiddle" to Aunti Em, he was not without importance. He, too, was a warm, loving individual, who tried to console Dorothy when Toto was going to be taken away "to be put to sleep." And he, too, was there at the end to greet Dorothy when she returned from her journey to Oz.

Well, I have memories of my own Uncle Henry, too. A burly, but soft-spoken and *heimish* individual, Henry was one of a Minyan of brothers who, with their parents, came to this country from Poland. I can still see him leaning back, looking out as he spoke, with the outer appearance of one commenting on momentous issues. Of course, he was, though these were not issues which would reach the news or be recorded in the tomes of Harvard's Widener Library. Because for Henry what transpired with the family and members of the community was the everyday momentous stuff of life.

Henry was well suited to the work he did, which was to fulfill the responsibilities of the associate director of *Chesed Shel Emes* in Detroit. *Chesed Shel Emes* is a funeral parlor for the Jewish community in my hometown. Now you may ask, "What is this unusual name for a funeral parlor? Couldn't there be something more easily pronounceable?" In fact, the name is entirely apt. For in Judaism we not only stress the importance of kindness in human relations, but take special note of those instances when the recipient is not able to do us anything in return. This is not only *Chesed*, or kindness, but *Chesed Shel Emes*, or pure, true kindness. Acting with respect and love toward the deceased is, thus, the quintessential act of *Chesed Shel Emes*. My Uncle Henry I remember for his embodying this virtue, after which his place of employment, his place of service, was named.

We at Mishkan Tefila are privileged in having so many who observe this same value. Among them is one who some months ago initiated a project which is praiseworthy in the highest and which, certainly in my experience, is a first. Growing up in Chelsea and attending Congregation Shaare Zion (the "Orange Street Shul") in that same community, one of our distinguished members, Lenny Florence, developed ties which have remained with him throughout his life. While moving on and becoming a leader in the world of business, Lenny nevertheless made a point of attending at least one service a year at Shaare Zion, and when the synagogue was about to close, because of declining membership, he decided that steps must be taken so that its departed were never forgotten. With the help of two of the final members, Rosalie Krakofsky and David Chase, and in consultation with the ninety-four year old retired sexton, Reuben Bunick, now deceased, records were amassed which would enable Kaddish to be recited on the appropriate day for each of the departed of Shaare Zion here at Congregation Mishkan Tefila.

I feel honored that I was called upon to recite this prayer in memory of people whom I never knew, but with whom we are all bound as members of the Jewish people and through our fellow humanity. Information is being further organized and recorded so that relatives of the departed will know that their loved ones are being remembered at a sister congregation. Our heartfelt thanks are due to Lenny Florence, who, by his example, teaches the value of *Chesed Shel Emes*, of kindness without strings attached. I am sure that from his place in another abode my Uncle Henry would say *Yashar Koach*, a job well done!

Postscript: With red face I must now confess to a mistake made in the above article. In a phone call with my brother, Phil, last night I recalled that it was actually my Uncle Nate who served as associate director of *Chesed Shel Emes*. Furthermore, said Phil, Henry is the one uncle who is still alive. So, I really goofed—and in an article on remembering, no less! (I wouldn't be surprised if Henry felt like Mark Twain who, in response to the premature announcement of his death, said in a cable to the Associated Press, "The reports of my death are greatly exaggerated.") Still I feel certain that each uncle—from his respective address—gives a hearty *Yashar Koach* to Lenny Florence. And so, too, I bet, does Dorothy's Uncle Henry—like all *heimish*, caring folks. *Yashar Koach*, Lenny. *Yashar Koach*—from us all!

A ROCKING CELEBRATION AT THE MISH

In the "Sim Shalom" prayer we thank God for having given us "a Torah of life and the love of kindness." Perhaps, however, these two things should not be regarded as two. Perhaps kindness is the chief quality which the Torah wants to teach us. Interestingly, the Talmud often refers to the Torah as *Rachmana*, which means, "the Merciful One." This, as you might guess, is a name for God, from which it follows that the Torah is regarded as communicating the very essence of godliness. To be godly is to be merciful or kind.

Now we at Mishkan Tefila have organized our programming this year around the threefold theme of Torah study, worship and the performance of deeds of kindness. But perhaps these three things should not be regarded as three. The study of Torah is meant to direct us toward the performance of deeds of kindness. And when we pray, we call upon God as the very source of kindness in the world. The mind which studies, the heart which prays, and the face which smiles to cheer up a fellow human being are all aspects of one person.

We, therefore, extend to you this hearty invitation to come to our combined Hanukah and Hanukat HaTorah (Dedication of the Torah) Celebration on Sunday, December 5, from 10:30 A.M. to 12:00 noon, in the combined sanctuary-lounge area. There we shall commemorate and rejoice in the victory our ancestors won for the observance in freedom of Judaism. And there we shall dedicate a newly repaired and restored Mishkan Tefila Torah scroll.

The scribe who has performed this work for us, Rabbi Simon Miara, will be on hand to pen in the final words, making our scroll complete. Rabbi Miara has also been meeting with students to instruct them in the mysteries and techniques of the scribal art. Remember: THE TORAH YOU RESTORE MAY, IN TURN, RESTORE YOU. (Contributions can still be made to the congregation, earmarked for the "Torah Restoration Project," to cover the costs of the scribal labor involved in repairing our Torah and in teaching our young people.) So, don't forget—December 5th at the Mish.

It'll be a rocking celebration!

A BALONEY SANDWICH IN HEAVEN

You know, we Jews have a great tradition of commentary on texts from the ancient to the contemporary. In earlier times the comments were normally inserted in the margins of the original text. Now scholars and critics prefer the essay-style, writing independent discourses on material which captures their interest. In the following article I have adopted a method closer to that of our forebears, presenting four brief texts, with immediately attached comment and discussion. The first two concern individuals in the fields of humor and medicine and are reworkings of accounts provided by them, whether through phonographic record or person-to-person communication. The final two are autobiographical, episodes from my own life.

Text Number One deals with the illustrious comic and sage, Steve Martin. It describes an afterdeath experience, which he returned to report.

I awoke to find myself in another realm. There was a mist, and through it I could see a throne. It was the throne of the Divine King. Suddenly, a voice called out, 'Bring him forth!' Two angels ran up and began to drag me toward the throne. I shouted, 'Wait a minute! Wait a minute!' The angels responded, 'What do you mean, 'Wait a minute'? You're going for your eternal judgment!' I shot back, 'I know. But in college they said this was all baloney!'

Now what do we learn from this passage? We learn, first, not to be so sure of ourselves. Sometimes we really think that we know what's what. But can we prove it? And will our proof hold up before further evidence? Just a century ago scientists thought they had the universe mostly figured out. And then came along little Albert Einstein (he was only in his twenties) to blow up their certainty with his Theory of Relativity. From a religious point of view the human heart can point us to ultimate truths, like the truth that life has eternal meaning and morality is a divine command, not just a personal feeling. Our human reason is limited. Faith is also part of the picture.

Which leads me to Text Number Two. This concerns our own Dr. Abraham Zimelman, from the days of his childhood in Argentina.

The cantorial candidate ascended to the lectern and began his chanting. He had a quite good voice, but there was something strange about his singing. It was Shabbat, and he was singing the prayers to the music of the festivals. At the kiddush following the service little Abe and his father went up to greet the cantor. 'Gut Yontif!,' sang out Abe, upon which his father gave him (Abe) a *pahtch* he never forgot.

Now what do we learn from this passage? We learn, first, that if human knowledge is limited, it's still important to know. Imagine trying out for a job and one of the Little Rascals throws you a curveball during the interview. Knowledge is important, and music is, too. The music of our services creates a special feeling. It helps the people get into worship and lifts them up. And the fact is that this can happen, too, with the simple, but moving chants of our weekday services. So, you can consider this an advertisement for my individualized course, "Synagogue Chanting Skills as Taught in a Little Red Schoolhouse." Call me at Mishkan Tefila, and we'll set up a special time when you can learn the weekday chanting, beginning with a five-minute stint and building up beyond that, if you wish. Faith is important, but music helps fuel it, too. And you can do it—if you only give yourself the chance.

Now Text Number Three.

It took place in Ann Arbor. I was living in a Jewish coop, called 'The Hebrew House.' One day, while reading a book, I went into the room of my friend, Phil Stein. Phil gave a look and said, 'Davin, I see you always with books. Is it true that ignorance is bliss?' To which I said, 'I don't know. But I'm happy!'

Now what do we learn from this passage? It's simple. Knowledge and joy can go hand in hand—even if you don't always know it! You may think that learning is drudgery. Or it's too dull or difficult. But it's not. Humility is great, but I've seen all these self-doubters who get up and do a bang-up job. And you can, as well. The appreciation from the people will be overflowing, as will your own good feeling. Try it. You'll definitely like it. Call today.

And now, Text Number Four.

Many years ago I took a High Holiday pulpit in a small Connecticut town. At its height there were only fifty people in attendance. Accidentally, I got to the end of the Yom Kippur prayers too early. We couldn't blow the Shofar yet, and I was afraid that we wouldn't have the requisite Minyan when the time arrived. So, I began telling the congregation Hassidic tales and, in fear at our declining numbers, ones with a humorous twist. At the conclusion of the service I told the people how much I enjoyed singing and speaking in their congregation. A fellow from the back called out, 'We really liked your monologue!

Now what do we learn from this passage? It's simple. PARTICIPATION. The man got involved, if not necessarily in the most socially appropriate way. And we want your involvement here. Come to the Minyan. Come to the little Red Schoolhouse. Come to Adult Education. PARTICIPATE. And give us your own commentary on your unfolding experience here at Mishkan Tefila. We will be eternally grateful.

FOOTBALL AND FAITH
A Life with Lions and Tigers

My father and I exited the stadium early, trying to beat the crowd which would follow the certain defeat one Sunday of our hometown Detroit Lions. We turned on the radio to hear the bad news, and lo and behold, the star quarterback, Bobby Layne, brought the team back in the last two minutes to a startling—even unbelievable—victory. That was the last time we ever left a game early, as over and over again Layne pulled off his feat of a come-from-behind victory in the waning minutes of the final quarter.

Memories of those childhood days came back recently when I bumped into Alexander Kuritnik, father of current Hebrew school student, Michael, and of former Bar Mitzvah student, Boris. For Boris I used to call the "Bobby Layne of my Bar Mitzvah Students." Why? I'm sure you can guess. Boris did an outstanding job on his Bar Mitzvah, but for some time until the closing weeks of his preparation period, I didn't feel certain he would be ready. Then Boris poured on the steam and did a stellar job on his "big day." He taught me to realize that I never had it all figured out, that there were potentialities present even when the empirical facts seemed to suggest otherwise.

The confidence that there is more at work than we know, the knowledge that despair is an error as an ultimate stance toward life, is of the essence of faith. From the two Bobby Laynes of my life I learned something about this faith, which entails the decision to persevere even without external, supporting evidence. The evidence comes into view in response to the act of persevering. The survival of the Jewish people is a case in point. The survival of each person bent low by the searing pain of grief is another.

Today I wish to take a different tack in my article and comment briefly on a book I have read which touches on this central phenomenon of faith. It was recommended to me by our president, Dr. Barry Benjamin, and is a novel by one Yann Martel, called *Life of Pi*. Contrary to what you may expect, the mathematical concept of Pi plays no—or virtually no—role in this book. "Pi" is rather the nickname of a young man who finds himself in a lifeboat with a tiger, following the sinking of the ship on which they were both sailing. The feline creature was there as a zoo animal in transit, and now Pi must manage 227 days with him out on the ocean, until he arrives safely on the shores of Mexico.

The son of a zoo keeper, Pi has learned the tricks used by animal tamers to cow (oy vey, no pun intended!) a ferocious beast. With this knowledge, and his own wit and luck, he survives against all odds, only to be disbelieved by those who question him. In response to their skepticism, he fabricates an alternate story more acceptable to the rational mind. Still, as one of the questioners says, the first story is the better one. Pi responds that the same is so when we speak of God in our account of human life.

Now what does Pi intend by this? That God is only a fictional being, brought in to create the feeling that there is a deeper presence and source of hope in our lives, a feeling which is really only an illusion? I doubt that. I believe rather that in Pi's eyes life itself is more than a mundane affair, and even if God does not clobber us over the head with proof of His existence, there are clues which abound, and which should give pause to the one who specializes in doubt.

To mention some which come to mind, I would begin by pointing to the phenomenon of life itself. For in the light of modern science the universe seems in its fundamental physical make-up to be subtly constructed or fine-tuned so as to enable life to evolve. To many, myself included, this fine-tuning, to an extraordinary level of precision, points to a higher intelligence who formed the universe with life as an ultimate goal. The traditional name for this intelligence is, of course, God.

And then there is the pull of values which we feel we must serve, even though they may not aid us in any "practical" way. The attraction of knowledge for its own sake, even for many who seek new technological developments, is one instance of this. The compulsion which artists feel to create works of beauty, even if they do not sell, is another one. The subordinating of one's own interests to help another is a further example. For some reason human beings act, at least in part, like spiritual beings, creatures with a higher calling.

Beyond this, there is the sense that even with death the infinite meaningfulness of an individual does not die. A person is not simply a clod of earth which feels and thinks and acts and then expires, and that is all. A person is rather, as Abraham Joshua Heschel put it, the bearer of a preciousness which is eternal.

Finally, there is the act of faith itself, which may inspire us with hope and trust. Is it not outlandish that our journey as Jews began with a single individual, Abraham, hearkening to God's command to go forth from his homeland, without even being told what was his exact destination? Is it not unbelievable that his descendants, exiled for two-thousand years, returned to re-establish their homeland, embattled and tested as it is?

We have been on a lifeboat, facing a tiger. We have persevered—and we shall. What was to be rationally expected did not work out.

Pi would understand.

So would Bobby Layne.

UNCLE SIMCHA

I'm not sure how many "greats" go before the "uncle," but I believe it is five, which makes my ancestor, Rabbi Simcha Bunam of Pshischa, my great-great-great-great-great uncle. Simcha Bunam was an interesting man. While intellectually sophisticated, he knew how to put things in a down-to-earth way. A Hassidic scholar adept in Talmud and Kabbalah, he could communicate with the "man-in-the-street."

Once, in an effort to explain the Ten Commandments, Simcha Bunam noted that this compilation of teachings does not begin by referring to God as the Creator of the Universe. Would that not have been more appropriate when the Master of the Universe wished to establish His authority as the supreme lawgiver? To the contrary, Simcha Bunam believed.

At the moment when God has just finished liberating the Jews from slavery, speaking of something so cosmic and mind-boggling as creation would have been too much. Rather in saying, "I am the Lord, your God, who took you out of the land of Egypt, the house of bondage," God, in effect, said, "I am the One who fished you out of the mud. Now you come here and listen to Me." That is, God associated Himself with the nitty-gritty concerns of the people. He spoke to them where they were, in a way that would get their attention.

In a sermon I published dealing with the Exodus from Egypt I highlighted this teaching from my "uncle" for what it conveys about the Jewish religious vision. While affirming a God who transcends nature, it still emphasizes the importance of the everyday, the worldly, the "oh-so-human." And it utilizes means both august and homey for instilling its message. Thus, in our musical tradition, for example, we find both sublime liturgical compositions and *niggunim*, wordless tunes, emanating from the world of Hassidism, which emphasize the role of the catchy melody and the thumping rhythm.

Recently, while traveling to the synagogue to teach my Bar and Bat Mitzvah students, one such tune popped into my mind. I couldn't exactly place it. I believed it had some measure of originality, though the rhythms were familiar, perhaps taken from "here" and "there."

After a period of reflection I came to trust that I would not experience what I did some years ago when, in the shower, I discovered the origin of one line of music in a piece I had composed.

Singing my *niggun* to Cantor Finkelstein, I received confirmation that while it is not revolutionary from a musical point of view, it is new, and he wished that it be taught to the participants in the *Seudah Shlishit*, or post-Minchah repast, on Shabbat, March 25. Perhaps the nitty-gritty, here in the sphere of sound, can make a point, one which will hopefully be understood by the emotions, even if there is no accompanying text.

This sense of the down-to-earth emphasis of Judaism will, I am sure, be felt even more powerfully by me about one month later, at the time of Pesach. And that will be as a result of the honor I have received of leading a Seder this year at the Children's Hospital. Joining Dr. Frederick Mandell of the hospital staff, I will conduct the first evening Seder for hospitalized children and their parents. Who will learn more from whom? Might I, the leader, be inspired by the fortitude of those I meet in their own battle for freedom from illness? As Fred Lawrence, who has led such Seders for many years, said, such a concrete concern with liberation may be energized in both those who are afflicted and those who are touched by them through the means of the Pesach Seder.

The focus on the nitty-gritty, the down-to-earth, the concrete, is one we confront over and over in our lives as Jews. We seek God not only at special moments and exceptional occasions, but in the everyday. One is struck by the words recited during each Amidah, "We thank You and praise You morning, noon and night for Your miracles which daily attend us and for Your wondrous kindnesses." What are these miracles and kindnesses? They are not the splitting of the Red Sea or the propulsion of Elijah's chariot to heaven. They are the dawning of the day, the awakening to consciousness, the taste of new bread and the greeting of family member and friend.

It is my good fortune as your ritual director to enjoy a diversity of responsibilities, encompassing, with varying frequencies, the entire range of tasks performed by Jewish clergymen. Teaching, singing, speaking, composing English prayers and liturgical music, I feel honored at the breadth of opportunities in our congregation.

In the spirit of my "uncle," Simcha Bunam, I would have to say that the engagement with the nitty-gritty of our religious life is an honor and source of appreciation. How fortunate are we all to be among those to whom the Almighty said, "Now you come hear and listen to Me."

Part II

FROM HUCKLEBERRY FINN TO THE COSMIC HOTEL: A POTPOURRI OF PARSHANUT (INTERPRETATION)

"DO YOU HAVE A PERFECT MIND?"

It was the early eighties and I was in graduate school in philosophy at SUNY Stony Brook. One day in the library I bumped into a younger student whom I knew. He was Moslem, and as we moved from pleasantries into substance, he proceeded to tell me that the Koran was the absolute truth. Each time I said something which called this into question he provided me with a response which he believed disproved my point. If he could come up with no such response, he claimed that what I was presenting was simply "Western propaganda."

Finally, I decided to use his own religious approach against his fundamentalist faith. I asked him, "Muhammad, do you have a perfect mind?" Of course, he could not say that he did, for he would then be asserting that he was God. So, he said, "No." To which I responded, "So, you might be mistaken!"

Muhammad realized that he was caught and then blurted out, "But I must believe this, because my father told me it was so, and if I don't believe it, I will fall apart." The claim of certainty had an emotional base, the need to feel secure in a vision of meaning provided by one he loved and trusted.

Of course, Muhammad's dogmatism is typical of all fundamentalists and, in fact, all absolutists, both secular and religious. To a doctrinaire Communist empirical realities, much less moral crimes, could not call into question the truth of the Marxist path to social redemption. Hopefully an ability, at least when pressed, to achieve a measure of self-awareness, such as Muhammad showed, would serve as a break against any temptation to coerce others into one's view—or even destroy them.

We human beings do, indeed, have a desire to know, but true enlightenment concerning ourselves entails a recognition of the limits of our knowledge. Even if those we most trust tell us that something is so, that may not be the case. And that means that we cannot gain the security we want if we require intellectual certainty regarding the big questions of life. "How did the universe get here? What are we doing here? What happens to us when we die? What is the source of the moral feelings which pursue us in life?"

We can turn to the received answers of our society or family. But when we wake up from our childlike trust in the wisdom of parents and other authority figures, we realize that we are, to a degree, alone in our search, not because no one else is searching, but because everyone else is like us, lacking in certainty, lacking in absolute knowledge. Is there a way beyond the anxiety of uncertainty, the anxiety of wanting to be rooted in meaning, but knowing that no vision of meaning can be absolutely proven?

As I ponder this question, my thoughts go back to Annie Grober, an elderly cousin already at the time I recall her. Annie herself has already passed on, but at the time of my recollection she was helping out during the Shiva, or week of mourning, for my grandfather, Morris Stolsky, of blessed memory.

Annie had a natural helping way about her. It was not simply that she would bring in meals. Her manner, her voice, her expression all reflected a genuine concern for the wellbeing of others. In other settings I associate her naturalness with an almost childlike laugh, her response of pleasure at funny comments or occurrences during her interactions with others. Annie was connected in her *being* to others, and she cared for them at least as much as she cared for herself.

I once imagined Annie conversing with a philosopher of a certain type, that kind known as a relativist in the field of ethics. For a relativist there are no absolute moral truths. When we claim that something is good, we are simply giving expression to the beliefs of the society from which we come. The same goes when we claim that something is evil. So, for example, we might view as bad the sadistic causing of pain to another, but that is only our belief. There is nothing absolutely true about such a claim.

In my fantasy I "saw" a relativist explaining to Annie his position and her responding not with a counter-argument, but with befuddlement. She simply could not comprehend how one could say or believe such a thing. She did not refute the relativist's claim, but experienced it as an absurdity. As I now re-experience this fantasy, I think that under the circumstances Annie would probably offer the relativist something to eat. Perhaps he was just not feeling well.

Now what was the source of Annie's conviction, or certainty, if you will, that the obligation to respond, the obligation to care, is laid within us and not simply the product of societal belief? It was not intellect. It was rather the—heart. Annie was comfortable accepting that which could not be demonstrated to the satisfaction of the mind.

I do not mean that Annie would accept "any old thing" which one said. I simply mean that on an important matter like human interaction her secure belief stemmed from a source other than, and I believe, deeper than the reasoning mind. Undogmatic in manner and spirit, Annie found her guide in a place within, which eludes both demonstration and disproof by intellect and argumentation. Through this place Annie was not alone, but connected to others in a natural, felt way, which involved a sense of meaning, of value, in life.

While trained in philosophy, I find that, at times, my thoughts regarding God derive from an approach opposite to that into which I was educated. As a rational thinker, I might ask whether or not it makes sense to believe in God. If I see a way of answering this question in the affirmative, I might then proceed to pray.

For some time I have thought that it makes sense to believe in God because people pray. I do not mean that it makes sense to believe because praying people believe. I mean that praying powerfully conveys itself as an act which has not simply a human source. Praying "comes across," if you will, as an act in which people relate themselves to ultimate meaning, as if some source of ultimate meaning is present within them and moving them to pray. This stance, called prayer, announces itself, as does great music, as an intimation of and introduction to ultimate meaning.

Can I prove this? Of course not. But I do not believe this simply because I was told it was so. In fact, I was not so told. I realize further that sometimes we are convinced of things concerning which we might be mistaken. We might then feel that the only way ahead is through a "leap of faith," a commitment to that which escapes demonstration.

Without ruling out the role or legitimacy of this path of choice, I would counsel also a listening with the heart. What are those experiences which do not prove, but seem to open us up to a spiritual dimension within—and within which we perhaps dwell?

The Renaissance philosopher, Pascal, said that, "the heart has reasons which reason does not understand." If you are not sure why you should come to shul, I would suggest, do it! When you pray, you will perhaps find yourself in a "land" where praying is as natural as breathing the air and the song of the heart may be heard like the wind of the swaying trees.

"AND WHEN THE WORLD GOES KAPUT"

I was at the time the cantor of Temple Shalom of Milton, Massachusetts, and we had just about reached the end of the Shabbat morning service. It was time for the concluding hymn, "Adon Olam," or "Sovereign of the World," and we chose for this week a bouncy tune one would more likely associate with a "trip" on a merry-go-round.

Hearing it people might feel the impulse to clap their hands and swing back and forth rather than rivet their attention on the hymn's central theme of the eternal God who is, at the same time, close to one in times of trouble. With a tune like this, people would hardly be thinking about their problems. The music itself would send worry and anxiety packing, at least so long as one sang one's lungs out to the zesty melody.

And I must say that as the leader of congregational singing I had a hard time remaining serious, in particular when one member, about two rows back and clearly in my line of vision, began swaying and swinging and bouncing in his seat, roaring out the tune and beaming out a smile visible at least to Mars. In truth, I had to stifle a laugh which pushed hard against the muscles of my cheeks and barely succeeded as we finally reached the concluding words, "The Lord is with me, I shall not fear."

Now there is something which I find amazing about the "Adon Olam," which stands out all the more when it is sung to a high-energy tune, such as I described above. And that is the condition of the universe referred to in the third line. More precisely, it is the condition of there no longer being a universe, as the line reads, "And when everything shall cease to exist, He (God), alone and awesome, shall reign."

Now, of course, we might ask what it means for God to reign when there is nothing around over which He can reign. But perhaps the author (anonymous, by the way) simply means that God is inherently majestic, suitable, by nature, for reigning. This is so even if nothing exists, which in His kingly essence, He can direct and govern.

But is it not shocking that the future nonexistence of the universe is asserted in the "Adon Olam?" I tried to get this point across once while elaborating on it at a Tikkun Leil Shavuot (or all-night Shavuot study session). I sang the beginning of the line in question to the following translation, "And when the world goes kaput..." Of course, it would have been more precise had I sung, "And when the world goes poof..." For the "Adon Olam" is not simply talking about the world getting out of kilter, but rather of its vanishing into nothingness. *What is the point of creating a world if it is going to dematerialize? Is there a point to existence if existence ceases?*

I believe there are two possible ways out of this problem. The first would focus on the Hebrew word referring to ceasing, or *kichlot*. Interestingly, the root for this word in other contexts denotes a coming to completion. So, for example, at the end of the story of creation, we read in Genesis 2:1, *"Vayechulu hashamayim veha'aretz vechol tzeva'am,"* or "The heaven and the earth and all their array *were completed."* The world was not finished off in creation. It was begun. So, similarly perhaps the "Adon Olam" can be taken to be referring to a time not when the world ceases, but when it reaches perfection. Perhaps it refers to a time when life, in a morally realized form, really takes off, that is, a Messianic age.

On the other hand, the belief in a Messianic age is compatible with the notion of the physical universe as we know it ending. In such a conception that which is present at creation ceases, while a new form of existence arises. Perhaps these two forms are not entirely discontinuous, but are rather related like a butterfly to its preceding caterpillar. Or perhaps the transformation is even more radical than this. So, it is as if everything that we can think of when we say "everything" really does cease. Still its successor is not nothingness, but something we can barely even conceive of now. God then does have that over which He can reign, something too wonderful for us to picture at present.

While stimulating and uplifting, this interpretation of the words, "And when everything shall cease to exist," seems overly specific, as well as perhaps too positive in what it portrays. The emphasis in the "Adon Olam" is upon trust in the God who is with us even when things are awfully bad. And against this background the trust in a God who is an undying source of meaning is heightened when one speaks of meaning even in the face of the death of the universe. This journey called life makes sense. The cosmic journey called the life of the universe makes sense. This play, if you will, was called into existence by a playwright, by virtue of whom it has undying meaning—even if there is a last act.

But how does it have meaning? Must it not have an eternal impact beyond serving as a source of inspiration or reflection in the "memory-bank" of the Almighty?

It seems to me that the affirmation of God in the "Adon Olam" involves a conviction as to a meaning transcending our understanding. To simply serve as a means of enrichment for God's inner life does not seem like enough. To have faith in God is to have faith that there is an impact which would make sense to us if we could but grasp it, though, of course, in making such an assertion we are involved in a contradiction. For it is of our very nature that we cannot break through to such infinite understanding. Of our very being, we cannot grasp the full significance of our being.

Perhaps we should say that there is a meaning which is real and undying, and which we would clearly not regard as insufficient. God did not simply create the world in order to enhance His own mental or emotional life. There is a point He had, and in our existence we serve that point, in a way whose significance is unending. Thus, whatever happens in—or to—our world, we and our world *go on in meaning.*

The great American philosopher and psychologist, William James, wrote in the conclusion to his work, *The Varieties of Religious Experience* the following,

> God's existence is the guarantee of an ideal order that shall be be permanently preserved. This world may indeed, as science assures us, some day burn up or freeze; but if it is part of his order, the old ideals are sure to be brought elsewhere to fruition, so that where God is, tragedy is only provisional and partial, and shipwreck and dissolution are not the absolutely final things.

Did the author of the "Adon Olam" project a physical universe radically transformed? Did he rather expect a complete end to this universe, home of our bodily existence? Whatever he foresaw, or believed to be on the distant horizon, the author of this hymn, was confident that he—that we—are not alone. Our actions are not for nought. Our lives have an impact—wherever that may be—which is unceasing.

And so, we may each say... no better, we may each sing out, "The Lord is with me, I shall not fear."

Yes, I shall not fear!

BASKETBALL AND THE BIG BANG

According to conventional belief, the Torah came into existence when it was transcribed by a human hand. In the eyes of tradition, this hand belonged to Moses, who recorded the foundational work of Jewish life during an encounter with God at Mt. Sinai. The encounter actually involved the entire Jewish people, who were, however, too "blown away" by the power of the divine presence to "hang in there" and listen to most of the work being dictated. This job fell to a single man who had the inner strength to hear the divine word without becoming overwhelmed or undone.

Now according to the nontraditional, but religious, approach of many moderns, the Torah did not come into existence all at once. Rather it was written in phases, with many human hands participating in its creation. The text that resulted may still be revelation *in toto* or perhaps only in part. But in either case, it is not revelation in a single moment—or stretch of forty days. Centuries encompass the process through which the Torah came finally to be formed.

What unites the above approaches, from the most to the least traditional, is the belief that the Torah came into being in historical time. Whether the Torah was fully crystallized twelve hundred years before the common era or less than five hundred, it was during the human journey upon this earth that it got born. Now what is fascinating is that in Jewish mystical belief the Torah, in fact, existed before this journey began, before the Jewish phase of it began, before Abraham received his call or Moses was selected for his mission. The Torah predates the universe and as such had an existence which was not physical in form.

This Torah, not written on parchment, served as the very "floor-plan" according to which God created the world. It provided the spiritual outline which became embodied in the world. If we could look beneath the surface of the Torah we have, we would discover this Torah from on high. And if we could look beneath the surface of the world as it appears to us, we would discover this Torah, as well. It is, if you wish, the inner essence of the outer material reality we perceive.

Davin Wolok

A lighthearted story is told to convey this idea of a Torah which preceded the universe. As it suggests, God one day decided to engage in the act of creation, and like any good executive, set off to his office to issue the orders which would realize His plan. When He got there, He sat down at His desk, where the Book of the Torah was lying. He peered into it, but could not see anything, for the lights were out. Immediately, He called out to His assistant, "Hey, Joe, let there be light." Joe flicked on the lights. The Almighty looked into the Book and said, "My God, that's just what I was supposed to say!"

Now even if we don't take this story seriously, there is a serious point to it, and that is that the world was not created in "any old way." It was not the result of an arbitrary act. Even God is, as it were, bound by ultimate principles, and while all-powerful, He is not a "wild man." The Torah itself indicates the necessity of God acting according to principle when it portrays Abraham as challenging Him concerning His intended destruction of Sodom and Gomorrah. How can He destroy the innocent with the wicked? "Shall not the Judge of all the earth act justly?" Even when God seems to command an anti-ethical act, even the most extreme, namely the murder by Abraham of his own son, Isaac, it turns out that God never really intended for this heinous deed to be realized. God's will may be inscrutable, but it is not evil. The Torah guides His act of creation and His behavior in the world He created.

When we turn to contemporary science, we discover the view that our world came into existence from an explosion, a "big bang," out of which all the matter of the universe emerged. This world, which contains both that which uplifts and that which morally perplexes, is governed by physical principles which are the result of that primordial explosion. The complexity of the world and the apparent "fine-tuning" it would have needed in order to be the kind of world in which life could arise might suggest the creative role of a God in shaping it. But still much occurs which we have difficulty squaring with the presence of such a divine being. How might the notion of a pre-existent Torah on high help us in dealing with this conundrum?

Amazingly enough, a story I read some years ago about a basketball star might be of benefit in tackling this issue. The player in question, whose name I unfortunately forget, was a hard competitor for his team. Still he noticed that at times during a game there

107

developed a special back-and-forth flow in the play between his team and their opponents. It wasn't just that each time one team moved the ball well, and the other team responded with equal dexterity. It was rather that the movement of the two teams came to be experienced as a kind of single movement, like a dance which involves and requires two partners.

At such moments there seemed to be a single flow, and the two teams were undividedly part of it. And at these moments the star in question realized that he couldn't care less who won. He didn't tell his teammates how he felt, as he didn't sense that they were tuned in to the flowing unity he experienced. But it seemed as real to him as anything that could be pointed to physically. It wasn't the players. It wasn't the court. It wasn't the backboard. It wasn't the ball. It was something both impalpable and gripping. Though these weren't his words, what he described sounded like an unseen dynamic flow, a living pattern of movement in which he, in which they all, even if unaware, participated.

In his work, *Death of the Soul: From Descartes to the Computer*, William Barrett writes that, "we are creatures who are haunted by the feeling that we have some spiritual destiny beyond the material order." Still he notes that there are times when we seem to experience a spiritual meaningfulness right here in the material plane. On those occasions the physical world no longer seems to be simply an impersonal realm or "indifferent universe." Our alienation from the world experienced as such will, he says, "be healed only if the universe is believed to have some meaning in harmony with our own spiritual and moral aims..." While an experience of the kind to which the basketball player in question refers is not one of which Barrett speaks, it does, I believe, contain that quality to which he alludes, namely, of a spiritual dimension within the physical.

In our ordinary perception we see ourselves as separate. True, we share the air that fills the space between us, and through gravity our bodies are slightly drawn toward each other. But nothing, in our very being, unifies us. That is, unless in certain experiences, such as that of a unitary flow on a basketball court, we touch an underlying reality, which but waits to be realized in our common action and conscious awareness. Might we think of this as an aspect of that mystical Torah to which we referred above, a hidden principle in reality, a pattern, an energy, which lurks behind or within the veil of physical externality. Can one on a basketball court discover a living truth which is present throughout reality? For if it is truly spiritual, should it not "refuse" to restrict its presence to only certain specially sanctified domains? At the conclusion of the priestly blessing, which we bestow upon our children each Sabbath evening, we read, "May He (God) lift up His face unto you and grant you peace." Sometimes I have fantasized God, as it were, looking up from His desk and through the radiance of His face enveloping us in peace. Peace, togetherness, fellowship, dynamic unity—these are not all that we encounter. But at least at times, do these not seem like intimations or aspects of something eternal?

In the beginning was the big bang.

But perhaps on a basketball court, too, our cosmology, our conception of the origin and nature of the universe, may receive holy completion.

Face to face with you, I may see not a fighter, but a—friend.

BIBLICAL PSYCHOANALYSIS
A Case of "Traditional" Parshanut

When we think of psychoanalysis, begun by Sigmund Freud, our concern is normally with an individual who is undergoing treatment for disturbances in his or her own experience and behavior. The goal of such treatment is practical, the liberation of the person from irrational thoughts and painful feelings, from impulses difficult to control and inhibitions which are excessive. But technique alone, for example, the utilization of free association, is not sufficient to effect the cure sought. There is, after all, a theory concerning the inner psychological structure of a person, which illuminates the material brought forth through free association. Freud was a mapper of the conscious and unconscious mind, not only a doctor who sought to eliminate experiential and behavioral symptoms.

The concern of the Torah, we might think, is radically other than that of Freud. Its portrayal of dynamic characters might suggest ideas about our underlying psychological make-up, but clearly it does not present a theory of the mind, a psycho-analysis of its own. But as Rabbi Aryeh Wineman has explained, the Hasidic tradition sees the Torah as symbolically providing us with an understanding of the inner life of every individual throughout time. Thus, the Torah not only contains an account of events from the past and is not only, as Jewish mystics also teach, a symbolic text hinting at the underlying spiritual structure of the world as a whole. It is, as well, a narrative tapestry whose inner purpose is the disclosure of the soul-life of every person. Following the Hasidic approach I would like to examine the Torah's account of the first day in the story of creation as, in fact, a lesson concerning the inner structure of the human soul, a teaching about the diverse and yet intersecting forces at work in our experience and behavior.

The Torah begins its account with the words, *"Bereshit bara Elohimeit hashamyim v'eit ha'aretz,"* "In the beginning God created the heaven and the earth." In Jewish mysticism, however, this statement may be taken to mean, "With *reshit*, with wisdom, God created the heaven and the earth."

Still what does this all have to do with the human soul? "*Shamayim*" and "*aretz*," "heaven" and "earth," I would suggest, refer not only to the physical cosmos, comprised of higher and lower regions, but to two dimensions of the human being. The "*aretz*" or earthly dimension is not hard to understand. People have biological needs and urges. People have wishes to both defend and assert themselves as egos in a social context. In satisfying these inner wants and pushes, they may or may not commit any evil against others. But even if they do not, we do regard them as acting out of a fidelity to an exalted principle. "*Aretz*," is not the only dimension of a human being. People also have an urge to realize a higher purpose in their lives. They are attracted (not always, of course) by the ideal and respond to the call to realize a higher moral value, such as justice or equality. In this way they are characterized also by the "*shamayim*" principle, the heavenly principle.

Still why does the Torah say that it is with wisdom that God created these two principles or dimensions? The answer, I would suggest, is that out of the tension between them a fuller human existence may be attained. The Torah, a spiritual document, does not wish for us to negate or defeat the earthly principle within us, but rather to raise it up through the heavenly principle. Thus, the Torah views the joining of a man and woman in marriage, a union in which the physical dimension is not peripheral, as holy. Not by accident the rabbis came to call the ceremony in which they are joined *Kiddushin*, from the word for holiness. The ultimate Messianic vision of Judaism is not one in which we leave this earth for a purely spiritual plane, but rather one in which life on this plane is transformed in the light of the higher. God with wisdom created both "*aretz*" and "*shamayim*," for the sake of what could otherwise not be achieved.

The Torah continues, "*Ve'ha'aretz haita tohu vavohu vechoshech al pnei tehom ve'ruach Elohim merachefet al pnei hamayim*," "And the earth was without order, and darkness was on the face of the deep and the spirit of God hovered over the face of the waters." What does it mean to say that the "*aretz*" or earth was without order? Untamed by the higher, our biological and egoic urges are a jumble. One moment I want this, another moment that. My life is without unity. Impulses from inside are the decisive factor. And if I think that I have a rational

111

plan to aggrandize myself, perhaps I will ultimately discover that I have submitted to and been dominated by what is ultimately a self-defeating urge. So, for example, "Pride goeth before the fall."

What is the "*choshech*" or darkness of which the Torah speaks? This is the lack of understanding from which we suffer regarding our own inner selves. "*Hamayim,*" turbulent emotional waters boil up from within and we don't even know why we feel the way we do. Still at moments there is a feeling that we should be otherwise. At moments conscience, the voice of the "*ruach Elohim,*" "the spirit of God" gnaws at us. We need help out of the inner tumult, the incomprehension from which we suffer, mixed with pinpricks from a higher source.

The Torah then states, "*Vayomeir Elohim yehi or vayehi or,*" "And God said, 'Let there be light,' and there was light." That is, let the human being gain enlightenment regarding his own inner being. Let him attain self-understanding as an aid in the project of mastering his emotions and balancing the heavenly and earthly principles within. He will still be responsible for the choices he makes. He will still be responsible for utilizing his free will to act wisely and justly. But this task will be rendered more feasible when he understands why he feels pushed in different directions. Then he will be a subject deciding upon his own course of action, not an object bombarded from within by impulses he can barely control.

We then read, "*Vayar Elohim et ha'or ki tov,*" And God saw that the light was good." God saw that it was good having a being who could choose with awareness. God valued the risk involved in having such a being. For even with awareness, that being might still choose wrongly. Still God wanted a being who could choose, who was not a robot, but rather, like Him, blessed with free will. Such a being could rebel against God's own wishes, but if he was attentive to the light of understanding which God had made available to him, he could, if he so resolved, achieve a higher level of existence than that of an automaton. He could be like God himself, a free subject for whom moral action was a willed choice.

The Torah continues, "*Vayavdeil Elohim bein ha'or uvein hachoshech,*" "And God distinguished between the light and the darkness." Here one may become puzzled. If the light is a positive, why let the darkness, which is presumably a negative, remain? The answer is that while only darkness is not good, if all were unhidden, if all were seen in the light, that would not be good. But why not? The answer is that spontaneity of action requires that a person not engage in constant, all-pervasive self-examination. Yes, one must reflect upon oneself and train oneself in the good. But the training must be so thorough that one is finally, when the occasion arises, able to spring into action. That latter capacity is possible only when one is not always "looking over one's shoulder," asking if one is doing everything right.

While moral action transcends in importance how one functions in other spheres, the same principle is at work there, too. In sports, for example, one must, through practice, learn how to perform an act, such as swinging a bat, and then when the ball is pitched during a game, let loose and hopefully hit the ball. One must "be in the dark" about the functioning of one's body at the moment. Hopefully the proper way of moving will have by then been internalized and, thus, realized when needed. One must "be in the light" or aware of what is happening, but also "in the dark" as a result of earlier training.

Interestingly, even intellectual work requires at times "being in the dark," not only at the beginning when one does not yet know an answer, but even as part of the process of discovering the answer. A scientist or mathematician, for example, may work long and hard on a problem, but still needs time off when the part of her concerning which she is "in the dark," namely, her unconscious mind might wrestle with the problem. If she has worked hard enough, the answer might finally spring into the realm of the "light" or her conscious mind, even when she least expects it. Light and darkness are both valued by God and both essential in the entire spectrum of human life.

We then read, "*Vayikra Elohim la'or yom velachoshech kara laila*," "And God called the light 'day' and the darkness He called 'night'." Why does God name the periods of light and darkness? The answer is that by naming these periods He is highlighting their importance. They do not simply occur. They are to be singled out for recognition. And when their importance is recognized, we may more fully allow them to function in our lives. If, for example, we are living in a society, such as the contemporary one, where there is an excessive emphasis on consciously managing and controlling our environment, a recognition of the role of the "night" will help us to regain a more natural and spontaneous way of functioning. If we have come to overemphasize the need to give vent to impulse and emotion, a recognition of the importance of "day" will enable us to act with greater moral awareness and sensitivity. God names the light and the darkness because of their essentiality as facets of the full and balanced life.

The Torah continues, "*Vayehi erev veyehi vokeir yom echad*," "There was evening and there was morning, one day." Interestingly, the word "*erev*," or evening, is related to the word "*eirev*," or mixture. The word "*vokeir*," or morning, is related to the word "*bikeir*," which means to distinguish or differentiate. The Torah is teaching us that the heavenly and earthly principles in the human being must be joined. The vision of the ideal must guide our earthly behavior. Yet, the two must not be identified. We must not, for example, adopt the approach of some which attempts to identify the earthly or the natural with the divine. We do not view the instinctual as the ultimate. We rather attempt to sanctify it. In so doing we attain the oneness, the "*echad*"-reality, which is a human being in his fullness.

But why does the Torah speak of "*yom echad*," one day, rather than of "*laila achat*," one night? If both light and darkness, day and night, are affirmed, then why emphasize one side of the equation over the other? The answer is that while we recognize the role of the darkness or the night, the accent is ultimately on the liberation which comes when we hearken to that which is disclosed in the light, to the freedom which comes from fidelity to the truth, including the truth about ourselves. We do not attempt to stamp out that which remains hidden from the conscious mind. We do not attempt to extirpate either biological urge or healthy self-assertion. But we are bidden to guide these by a higher principle and a higher awareness.

May the psychoanalysis of the Torah illumine for us the fullness of our existence. May we seize the light and achieve our true stature as human beings, creatures imbued with free will and charged with the duty of using it for the sanctification of life in all its dimensions.

MY BUBBE IN THE COSMIC HOTEL

My grandmothers and great-grandmothers were a very wise lot. While they were not the beneficiaries of a higher education, they seemed to have powers of perception and understanding which are not the result of classroom learning alone. One, for example, had the critical eye of Sigmund Freud when it came to human motivation and behavior. As she put it in her earthy analogy, "Civilization is like the polish on a tarnished spoon." She naturally appreciated gentle and considerate conduct, but like the founder of psychoanalysis, did not believe that it flowed from an irresistible impulse in the human soul.

The consequences of a mass phenomenon such as World War I also did not escape her grasp. In her words, "World War I—everything changed." This recognition of the war's society-altering impact, at least in Europe, where she had lived, was derived by me only from the reflections of historians. True, I did not live in Europe—or anywhere on this planet! — during the time of which she spoke. But her ability to capture in simple terms the essence of a situation was not only the result of being on the scene. If insight is so readily available, then why do the "experts" so often disagree?

Now one of my great-grandmothers had both the reflective powers of a sage philosopher and the imaginative capacities of a first-class writer. She developed a conception of the world, taken as a whole, in which it was compared to a—hotel. We live, if you wish, in a *cosmic hotel*! What is the meaning of this image or association for our world? We don't book reservations before "checking in. "We don't plan an itinerary before "our bags are unpacked." We don't switch to another "hotel" if this one doesn't satisfy us. So, what is the meaning of the analogy which fails on so many counts?

It is this. A hotel is a temporary place of dwelling. We don't stay there forever. And unless it is "spanking new," we haven't been the first to remain for some brief period of time. Unless the hotel faces demolition, we will not be the last. The rooms, barring major renovation, stay basically the same. It is only the occupants who change. And so it is with our world. It has a durability and longevity in comparison with which we are temporary residents. It may have no more self-awareness than the bricks of the finest hotel. But it continues, at least for a very substantial period of time, while we, with our consciousness and sense of self-importance, pass on.

I do not say this to suggest that there is nothing of lasting importance in our existence. I do not even say that there may not be another plane where our existence itself, in a different form, continues. But even if that is so, our sense of importance concerning our ultimate status must be conjoined with humility. Here in this world we may conquer continents. But they remain, while we vacate the "rooms" which comprise them to make way for new occupants, for new "conquerors." Is there any way of tasting what might be of ultimate and eternal significance while we are yet in the "hotel?" Is there any way of seeing the "hotel" as not the whole story, even while we reside within it?

Our exploration of this issue will begin with an examination of a passage which might not seem to directly address the issue of meaning within mortal existence. True, it speaks of that which most people find deeply meaningful, namely, love. But it does not explicitly raise the question of mortality, which is of concern here. The passage is one of the most famous in the Bible. It is the injunction to love, to "love your neighbor as yourself."

It should be noted that this injunction is part of the final of two verses (Leviticus 19:17-18), which counsel against holding angry feelings within. One should express one's criticism of another in a non-destructive way. This is part of love, the source of which is God Himself. "Do not hate your brother in your heart; reprove your kin and bear no guilt on his account. Do not take revenge or hold a grudge against the members of your people, but love your neighbor as yourself, I am the Lord." Love involves honesty, but the kind which does not aim to tear your fellow person apart. His or her self-esteem must be as important to you as your own.

Now a question which arises when we read these verses closely is whether or not the injunction to love applies also to those who are not "members of your people." Are we instructed only to love fellow Jews? A major interpretation of the commandment to love, and the most widely accepted today, does not see it as pertaining only to Jews. But it must be admitted that this is neither the only interpretation which has been advanced nor the one which seems to fit the literal meaning of the text, taken by itself. It does, after all, explicitly mention the "members of your people."

Light may be shed on the Biblical command to love when we examine other related verses. Most strikingly the Torah, in the same chapter as that from which the above verses are taken, states regarding the stranger, or minority person, "love him as yourself, for you were strangers in the land of Egypt, I am the Lord, your God" (Leviticus 19:34). We should not imagine that a member of another people living in our midst is somehow foreign to us in his very essence. We can feel his feelings. We can see ourselves in him. We can see him, and must love him, as ourselves.

Now the above two commandments, to love the "members of your people" and to love the stranger, may be see as simply enumerating two groups to be loved, Jews and minority persons living amidst Jews. The Jew, however, in the first commandment is not seen simply as a member of a narrow ethnic group. For as the second commandment makes clear, any vulnerable person, any person who lacks a sense of permanence in our social world is likened to a Jew. Is there any way of feeling a likeness to all people, a spiritual identity, if you will, which does not negate difference?

In Leviticus 25:23 we read, "But the land shall not to be sold, with no opportunity of being recovered, for the land is Mine; you are but resident strangers with me." Amazing! No one is to regard the world, or any part of it, as his or her permanent possession. There is only one true owner. There is only one permanent resident—God. Between all of us humans there is a fundamental affinity, for we are *all* strangers in the world. We are strangers in the sense that we lack any absolute hold upon the place in which we dwell.

We human beings have been granted in the world temporary residence. If we but recognize this, our true status, we may be liberated from the impulse to "lay a trip" on others, to put them down so as to create the fantasy of godlike power for ourselves. If we realize that we are all here temporarily, we may be freed to love them, to love them as ourselves. To love the "members of your people" is a particularization of a universal principle, which is implicit from the beginning. The moral relations we should maintain with fellow Jews we should maintain with all people. For they are the same principles which humanity as a whole should observe in its quest for moral sanity and redemption.

I am not a believer in time travel, but if I were, I know whom I would like to meet, that Jewish philosopher, an elderly woman who accepted her condition with gratitude and humility. From her we learn that the world is not our private possession, but neither is it an abandoned building with no owner, with no one who is interested in the "goings-on" and the relations between the "guests."

My Bubbe had it right. The world is a hotel, God's cosmic hotel, and we should not "look down our noses" at our fellow temporary residents.

Let us make real love and compassion and sensitivity in the way we act toward others. They may, at first, seem strange to us, but looking closely we will finally see—ourselves.

THE GOD OF THE MASK

In Exodus 34:17 we read, *"Elohei maseicha lo ta'aseh lach,"* or "You shall not make for yourselves molten gods." Interestingly, the word for "molten" is *"maseicha,"* which may also mean a mask. The verse may, thus, be taken to saying, "Do not turn masks into gods for yourselves." What might this mean?

We might think that it is equivalent to the statement, "Do not engage in the worship of outer appearances," and certainly it should be understood to include this notion. For we are not to regard anything outward and superficial and fleeting, such as the images those in the media project, as of ultimate importance. But a mask is not a mere outer appearance. It is, after all, possible that the image a person in the news presents, in fact, reflects, at least in a fragmentary way, the real person.

A mask is an outer appearance that covers over or conceals the truth. Its intent is to hide, so as to make possible the perception by others of something not real. This may, of course, occur in an innocent way, as when people dress up for a Purim celebration. No one believes that Joe, the custodian, is really Ahashverosh, the King of Persia. And in any case, it would be somewhat difficult to knowingly idolize another if one believed that the outer appearance were but a mask.

The injunction against worshipping a mask may be directed against the feeling that one must present an outer image for others simply in order to become acceptable. To believe in a God who created each individual is to believe in the value of each individual as he or she is independent of some social formula as to what makes one "cool" or "O.K." As Rabbi Zusya noted, he would not be asked in the next world why he was not like Moses. Rather he would be asked why he was not like Zusya. There is a special appeal each person has by being true to his or her own real self.

In this way, we end up neither with a world of conformity, in which true meeting between individuals is undermined, nor with a world of self-centeredness, where each person is out for his or her own self. The varied richness of the human race is mutilated when we are called upon to sacrifice our uniqueness before the altar of the anonymous "they." We may ourselves be our greatest contribution to the human community.

Just as we are not to substitute any outer image for God, so we, in the image of God, should free ourselves from the believed need to win the approval of others by presenting a mask. The injunction to not "bend the knee" before the call to be a "successful personality" is an invitation to the freedom and peace of authentic selfhood. The fear of rebuff by the other is an inner demon. If a rebuff occurs, it can be tolerated. For the strength which comes from self-acceptance is not easily undermined by invalidation from without.

Do not feel that you must submit to the pressure to create a "face for others." Do not worship masks. They have power over you only so long as you believe in their necessity. Become yourself. The god of outwardness and mere appearance will wither before the confidence which true being emanates. The buoyancy of your inner spirit will be the reward for the courage to step forward as simply—yourself.

FROM "NOTHING" COMES MY HELP

In Psalms 121:1 we read, "*esa einai el heharim meiayin yavo ezri?*," "I lift up my eyes to the mountains, from whence will my help come?" The answer given in the next verse is that help comes from God, the maker of heaven and earth.

It is noteworthy that the word "*meiayin*," translated as, "from whence," may be understood in a different manner. If "*mei*" is read as a prefix, then the meaning of the word becomes, "from nothing." From nothing will my help come, says the Psalmist. What possible sense can be ascribed to such a statement by one who, at the same time, identifies God as the source of his help?

If "nothing" is understood in its usual sense, then, of course, no sense can be gleaned from this statement. But perhaps "nothing" need not be understood in its usual sense. For "nothing" may also be read as "no-thing." From no thing, from no worldly entity, no matter how impressive or "awe-inspiring," will my help ultimately come. Not from the possession of multitudinous material goods or things will I find ultimate security. Not from the attainment of great power or status, the cherished things of social striving, will I find emotional peace. No finite thing, which may vanish as easily as it came, will give me the help which I want most.

The security that "it all makes sense," that even in the face of the death of friends and loved ones and even in the face of the knowledge that I, too, shall die, still life has meaning, this security cannot come from any thing which I might obtain or come to own. I, the owner, do not own myself. I, the owner, cannot resist my return to the earth and to eternity, no longer to be a denizen of this world which I both fear and cherish. And if I, the owner, did somehow own myself, if I, the owner, could somehow repel any worldly force which could bring about my demise, would my unceasing worldly existence give me ultimate peace?

I wonder what is the meaning of my finite time on earth. But if I regarded myself as a mere accidental product of nature, with no ultimate purpose, with no higher, spiritual significance, would living for an infinite amount of time quiet my inner dis-ease? No thing, not even infinite time, will lift me up beyond my anxious concern for inherent worth.

Still the Psalmist, in our unconventional rendering of *"mei-ayin,"* does not simply say that from no thing will my help come. Rather he says that from no-thing, from that which is no-thing, my help will come. God, in this understanding, is not to be grasped as simply a greater or more amazing version of some thing or being which we may find in the world. God is not Superman. God qualitatively transcends every other being. As the source of the world, God is not an improved version of the things we find in the world. God is, as it were, *No-thing*, the *No-thing* by virtue of Whom the world exists and Who imbued it with a meaning whose presence we can sense, but which we cannot formulate in words.

Why does great music, which itself comes to an end, give us a feeling of unending meaning? Why do the leaves in autumn, about to fall, stir us with the sense of transcendent beauty? Why is the miracle of growth, which is not forever, a cause for rejoicing and celebrating? We know that one day we will mourn. Why is there hope? Why is sadness not the last word?

Even when we say that God is the source of ultimate meaning, meaning sensed in, but not explainable by, the world in which it is sensed, we have but named the source. The meaning is still ineffable. It cannot be formulated in words. If God were merely one more being or thing, possessing great or even infinite power, and had created us and the entire universe, still that alone would not explain the presence of meaning in existence. For God would still be just one more being, the one with extraordinary power. For a God of this kind, the universe could be nothing more than an experiment or plaything.

Our experiences point to a source of ineffable meaning whom we cannot adequately describe through any of our concepts. God is No-thing. From this one who is No-thing, from this one, my help comes. From Him come the intimations of eternal significance which carry us to the heights of the mountains—and even beyond.

I lift up my eyes. From the Nameless One, from No-thing, from God who created and transcends the world, I receive my help, wordless, beyond concept, beyond formulation.

Here, where nothing is said,
Here may No-thing be heard.

LEVINAS, HUCKLEBERRY AND THE ANGELS

The French Jewish philosopher, Emmanuel Levinas, is known, above all, for one idea. It is an ethical idea, and it concerns the other, not as we might conceive of him in solitary reflection, but as we encounter him, independent of pre-established interpretations and systems of explanation. Face to face with the other I am confronted by a call to respond. I am confronted by a call not in word or utterance. The need, the anguish, the vulnerability, the powerlessness in the face of the other are the very call which confronts me.

In this, the ethical relation with the other, I cannot look away — except willfully. And I cannot regard the call as a merely subjective experience, arising within me as a result of my training and education. Thus, through the ethical relation I become aware of God. Not that I have a direct experience of God, but rather that the other is, as it were, a trace of God, of one who transcends me and makes possible my being commanded. The call, the command, comes to me from the face of the other, testimony of a God who, if not present in Himself, is yet intimated in the ethical obligation with which I am confronted. God has, as it were, "been there," touching, making possible the face of the other, which is more than the outer surface of an object. The face in its anguish and vulnerability is a living soul who calls out and commands.

As I write of Levinas, I think of my hero, so dear to me, from American literature. He was no sophisticate, but in the purity of his heart, lived out that which Levinas sought to enunciate in his philosophy. He is so real to me that once, while teaching, I almost spoke of him as one of the most beautiful men in American history. Suddenly, in mid-sentence, I remembered that he had never lived, at least in the public spatio-temporal world which we call reality. His name is Huckleberry Finn.

Huckleberry, as we know, liberated his friend, Jim, from the clutches of slavery. He did not do so, however, because he had internalized an ethical principle which obligated him to act in this manner. In fact, he acted opposite to principle, opposite to the principle he had been taught, that to liberate a slave was sinful. Huckleberry saw Jim and had to respond. He saw Jim and could not not respond. I am not suggesting that Huckleberry was without free will. But to not liberate Jim would have required his active rejection of the demand which was laid upon him in his very face to face encounter with the man. Could he have regarded that as a mere subjective feeling? Could he have repressed his experience of a call? Of course. But to draw the blinds over a window does not mean that light is not trying to get through. The voice of my brother's blood cries out to me from the earth. To make my soul dead is not proof that no living being needs me. And to make my soul dead is not proof that God does not address me through my neighbor.

This linking of God and the relation with the other is powerfully suggested in the *Shacharit*, or morning, service, when it is said of the angels, "*vechulam mekablim aleihem ol malchut shamayim zeh mizeh*," "they all receive one from the other the yoke of the kingdom of heaven." What is this yoke? What is it quintessentially? It is the obligation to respond, to care, to not be able to turn away from the other, from his face which is before me. God here does not directly address the angels. He addresses them through each other. Is it that they are incarnations (in spiritual form, as they are angels) of God himself? No.

It is when one cannot turn away from an other who is not august and mighty, it is when one cannot turn away from the widow, the orphan and the stranger, it is when one cannot turn away from the slave, the untouchable, the one who is without power, that one has reached the ethical relation. In such a relation one does not become God. But one becomes godly. The angels in our prayer set an example for us. They each become angelic and holy in being turned toward the other, in hearing the other and stretching out a "hand" in response. It is here that the awareness of the divine is born.

O my friend, Huckleberry, thank you for living what Levinas sought to teach. Thank you for living what the angels on high embody. Thank you for being here, with your simple beauty, your unaffected kindness, your truth, not of words or of notions. Thank you for liberating Jim and for being liberated by him. May your relation draw us back to sanity, to harmony, and to peace.

IMMANUEL KANT— THE PSALMIST

In the preface to the *Critique of Pure Reason*, the eighteenth century philosopher, Immanuel Kant, makes a very disturbing—or liberating—comment. He writes that human reason, of its very nature, is compelled to ask questions which, of its very nature, it cannot answer. This is not to say that no answers can be given. But no proof may be found for the answers that we give.

Such is the case in many spheres of life. We are not sure whether a particular practical plan of action will work out or not. We feel uncertain in our assessment of another individual. We do not know whether a scientific theory will withstand the test of time and, in fact, believe that *in due time* it will not. If not refuted, it will be seen to explain only a limited range of phenomena rather than the broader domain it was assumed to account for. Ultimately, in a million years, or even a thousand or five hundred or less, it will be totally overcome—or at least may well be. No certainty is to be found in science or in everyday life, in the effort to explain how the world behaves or in the effort to behave in a way that works in the world.

But none of this may bother us as much as uncertainty in another sphere, and that is in the sphere of the "big questions." These are not simply the most far-reaching or fundamental questions we may ask. These are also questions concerning which uncertainty may beget anxiety. For example, "Is our being here a mere accident or is there a purpose and intention behind it? Is blind nature the ultimate 'ruler' or is there a Creator, a God, who willed our existence and has a meaning in its being pursued? How did the world get here? And if, as people once believed, it was always here, how come it doesn't just 'go poof?' Does it have a magical power within it which enables it to exist? I mean, I know something about how the world works. But couldn't there just as easily have been no world, neither this one nor any other? Yes, science explains, or tries to explain, the world that we've got. But it would do the same if the world were put together differently. Why this world? Why any world?

And why do I sometimes—or often—feel that there is a particular way I am called upon to behave, not because it is advantageous, but because it would be *wrong* to act otherwise? What is this strange quality of *rightness* and *wrongness* which may attach to actions? Where does it come from? Why do I sometimes—or often—act thinking only of my own interests and at other times feel pained if I see another in pain, almost as if his pain or hers were my own? Are we linked in some strange way, not telepathically, but like fellows in a community deeper than the plane of the visible? When I peer out at an other, and he at me, are there more than physical bodies present to each other? Are there selves not fully explainable physically? Are we spirits embodied, bearing an awareness as if, or in fact, from another plane, one which somehow pervades our own, but in a way which defies our comprehension? Can we ever get all of this straight? Can we get any of it straight? Can our reason give us the certainty which would grant us peace?

Kant's answer to this question is no. We can seek, but certitude eludes us. Absolute knowledge concerning the truth of the answers we give to the most fundamental of questions is an impossibility. And thus, the anxiety that is inherent in our condition. For the matters raised are not peripheral to the question of who we are. If we have an ultimate destiny, if the challenges we confront must be endured and struggled with for the sake of a purpose which both explains and is served by our existence, then our lives are radically other than if they have resulted only from a series of biochemical accidents on the surface of the planet, earth.

Thus, I ask, "Who am I? Who am I down-deep, not simply as a member of this society, but even if I were born centuries before or centuries hence? Why are we here, and is there any ultimate purpose in our meeting? When we say 'hello,' do we each greet a being of infinite meaning? When we say 'good-bye,' even for good, is there an infinite significance, an eternal value, in our having met and 'been there' for each other?" These are the questions that burn in our heart and from which we cannot hide, unless we have fled from our souls— or they from us. These are the questions which will not die—unless our soul has died within us.

And so, even if I should seem overwrought in an age pacified with explanations on the surface, I will not prevent these questions from possessing me. I, therefore, cry out and ask you to answer me. Or join me in pursuing together an answer. Meet me and perhaps the love of friends which is awoken between us will be an answer in a universe in which "there is no utterance and there are no words, the sound of them is not heard." Or is this perhaps, is the silence itself, the voice of One who is present—but beyond sound? Do we confront a void or a stillness which quietly speaks? Free me from doubt. Let me know that You are here, You, O Nameless One, Perplexer of minds, a Friend who self-conceals—for the sake of the search? For the sake of the journey?

Thus saith the Psalmist Kant, "The heavens are the heavens of the Lord, and the earth He has given to the sons of man (Psalms 115:16)."

We here on earth ask questions that cannot be answered from within the limits of our reason. But let us ask. Let us ask and regard our questioning—and answering—as a response to the Silence which is neither barren nor empty.

In peace, let us join together.

WHO IS PRAYER?

Sherm left the hotel and headed straight for his car. He had a long trip ahead of him, and it was an unusual trip. Or at least that's what it would have been for most people. For Sherm was on his way to say Kaddish in a shul—*two-hundred miles away*! Two-hundred miles away? Yes, indeed. That's where the nearest shul was, and nothing would stand in Sherm's way when he intended to say Kaddish for a loved one.

I learned of this while sitting on the bimah of Temple Shalom of Milton, Massachusetts, looking out at members of the Boston Red Sox community and listening to one of the eulogies given in Sherm's behalf. The man of whom I am speaking was Sherm Feller, the late announcer for games at Fenway Park, and as cantor of Temple Shalom, I was waiting to chant the *El Maleh Rahamim* memorial prayer at his funeral.

Now, as I have suggested, Sherm's journey on behalf of a Kaddish would have been unusual for most people. But for Sherm, or someone like him, it should have been even more unlikely. For Sherm was in almost every other respect a non-observant person. His funeral took place at Temple Shalom, not because he was a member of the shul, but because his sister was. Sherm was, in fact, not a member of any shul. But member or not, he could not forget a loved one and believed that the act of remembering required one's full and absolute commitment. Thus, he could drive two-hundred miles for a Kaddish, and if necessary, would have driven a hundred more.

If I say that Sherm was a people person, I don't mean simply that he could interact easily with others. My guess is that he could, though I never had the privilege of meeting him. But he clearly was a people person in the sense that people mattered deeply to him. What most might regard as an excessive demand, he saw as both a duty and a personal desire. What most might see as "too much," he saw as just what was required for the occasion. Sherm sanctified God's name through his acts of loving remembrance. In doing these he lodged his name indelibly within the minds of all who knew him or heard of him.

The emphasis on action, so manifest in Sherm's life, brings to mind the teaching of a Hassidic rabbi, which I learned of from the writings of Martin Buber. It is not that Sherm had the same belief orientation as the person—or kind of person—concerning whom the rabbi was questioned. Sherm, I suspected from the words I heard, was a believer, even if one who did not, by and large, maintain traditional observance. The rabbi, in the text which Buber brought, was asked why God permits there to be atheists in the world. Could He not have prevented people from having this belief, or non-belief, orientation? The rabbi answered that a believer might say, on witnessing a person in need, that God could help him. An atheist would have no alternative but to aid the person himself. God wants action, and atheism might prompt the action which God seeks.

With this thought in mind, I believe it is possible to see a new meaning in the opening words of the line in liturgy which reads, "May my prayer to You, O Lord, be in an acceptable time." For these words, "*Va'ani tefilati lecha*," can also be taken to mean, "May I be my prayer unto You." In other words, the person is asking that he himself become a prayer, that he himself become that which he offers unto God. Not words alone may be that which we raise up to the Almighty. Acts of lovingkindness, too, acts in which the feelings of others matter and they themselves matter, even when no longer here, such acts may be the clearest form of service to God. Such acts, though lacking in any verbal affirmation of God's existence, may nonetheless speak of the presence of God in the human soul and in its comportment toward the souls of others.

The British rabbi and thinker, Louis Jacobs, in fact, claims that the behavior of certain atheists is itself a powerful argument for the reality of God. While asserting that there is no higher foundation to ethics, they themselves act as if certain things are absolutely forbidden to us. To humiliate another, to abuse another, to torment or sadistically cause pain to another, is impermissible. But why? If there is no higher source of ethics, then why can't one do such terrible things simply because one wants to? Conscience is the voice of God within. Those who feel for others, and act on this feeling, testify to God's reality. Their life is itself a prayer to God, even if unconscious of the One to whom it gives praise. Through action one's life may become worship. Through action one may answer the question, "Who is prayer?," with a human name.

Somewhere in the next world, I trust, a service is under way, and the one announcing the pages and guiding the participants is a man for whom distance meant nothing when love and memory were at stake. In this way he earned his spiritual leadership. In this way he earned his place in our soul forever.

HONEY AND THE SAINT

When I speak of Elijah, I don't mean the figure from the Bible. But like him this one, too, was righteous. I don't mean that he "laid it on thick." I mean that in his everyday relations, in his actions toward people in the ordinary circumstances of life, he revealed a moral character which could only be described as righteous. He knew what people felt, and he responded to them before they even put their feelings into words. He could look at a human face and say what the person needed to hear before he voiced his need in audible terms. He was sensitized to the soul of others and made them feel welcome through his preemptive goodness.

Elijah knew how lonely it could be to be a young person in town without a family and sought to make others feel like they were part of his family. And so, he had the wonderful habit of inviting young people over for lunch, where they could feel that they were on the receiving end of warmhearted interest, respect and friendship from a member of the older generation.

Marrying into a family which prizes remembrance, I learned of Elijah because he is my great-grandfather-in-law. To be more specific, he is the father of Bertha, who is the mother of Shifre, who is the mother of Carol, to whom I am married. And the little tale which I wish to relate involves Elijah and Bertha and a number of young men whom he invited over one Sunday for a midday meal.

The men enjoying Elijah's hospitality on the day in question were from the same town in Poland from which Elijah had come. And here they were in Woodbush, South Africa, not feeling marooned in a foreign country, but meeting up with an already established gent from their home country. As they came into Elijah's house, the men placed their hats, top down, on the table in the entrance hall. The hats would be waiting for them when several hours of good food and conversation had gone by.

But Bertha, O Bertha, a daughter in search of naughty delight, had something else in mind. Not that the hats would disappear between the arrival of the young men and their departure, but that an alteration of some sort would occur during this interval. And so, when the men came in and Elijah and they relaxed around the table, Bertha quietly made her way into the kitchen cabinet, from which she removed a glistening jar of honey.

Had it been Rosh Hashanah, perhaps Bertha could have justified the exploit in which she was about to engage by saying that she had only meant to sweeten the men's High Holiday experience. But she was without such luck. She simply had to rely on the gumption billowing up out of her own hearty spirit. And so, taking the jar of honey, Bertha stealthily made her way to the entrance hall. Upon her arrival there, she deposited a generous dose of honey into each man's hat.

Well, the lunch and the conversation finally came to an end, and the men headed toward the entrance hall in order to retrieve their hats. As each put his on, he had a strange, "gluey" experience, as the hat mushily, but unmistakably, stuck to his head. What was this? Had someone introduced a foreign substance into his quite proper headgear? Indeed she had, and Bertha was quickly uncovered as the culprit who had caused her saintly father such profound embarrassment. By contrast, the story of the hats with the honeyed inner icing has, over the generations, been a catalyst for chuckles and laughter, as you might guess from my having learned of it so long after its occurrence. What frustration and exasperation a righteous person may have to contend with in attempting to realize his dedication to his fellow human beings.

Now, interestingly enough, as Bertha matured she began to manifest, in abundance and intensity, her father's own qualities of goodness and sensitivity. She became involved in setting up a soup kitchen for needy black children in Pietersburg, the town in South Africa to which the family had moved and where she raised her family. She helped to establish a meeting place for unmarried pregnant women, so that shame would not be the only feeling which they would experience as members of society. When there was no rabbi in town, she engaged in providing the Jewish children with a Jewish education herself. And during World War II she worked in a women's auxiliary, providing refreshments to soldiers who were on their way to fight in North Africa. The prankster who foiled her saintly father's goal of a smooth and pleasurable lunch for lonely young men became a person of righteousness and strength herself.

These qualities, I believe, played a role in one young man named Sam becoming attracted to her and in their getting married. Sam was not only an honest businessman, though that, too, is an accomplishment worthy of mention. Sam was an unbelievably charitable man. In fact, this was so much the case that when he died the extent of his generosity exceeded even the most wild expectations. For Sam combined charity with modesty, givingness with a disdain for self-advertisement.

Now these thoughts of people who became part of my past when I married Carol awaken within me as I reflect on some of the most stirring verses I have read in the Book of Psalms. They are verses 19 and 20 of chapter 118, complex in construction and endlessly rich in meaning. Speaking in enthusiastic tones, the Psalmist calls out, *"Pitchu li sha'arei tzedek; avo vam odeh yah. Zeh hasha'ar ladonai; tzadikim yavo'u vo."* "Open for me the gates of righteousness; I shall enter through them and thank the Lord. This is the gate unto the Lord; the righteous shall enter through it." Let me briefly explore these verses, so moving, with you.

I would begin by noting that the first word of the translation, "Open," does not adequately convey the context in which the Pslamist speaks. For the Hebrew in this instance, *"Pitchu,"* is a plural term, meaning that a multitude is being addressed. A single individual is crying out, "Open for me the gates of righteousness..." Who is being addressed? One would guess that it is his fellow human beings, his parents and teachers and other role-models who are being asked to facilitate for him a passage through "the gates of righteousness."

And these "gates," what are they? I would assume that they are not physical gates. For in what way could gates of metal or wood or any other material be considered "gates of righteousness?" And if they were, why would an individual need more than one such gate in order to come before the Lord (in the temple?) to offer Him thanks? And why in the verse 20 are all these gates suddenly referred to in the singular? "This is the gate unto the Lord; the righteous shall enter through it."

In the passages we are considering a single individual calls out to the community to aid him in his quest to live the life of righteousness. And he recognizes that this path has many facets. Honesty, generosity, kindness, compassion are all elements of it. The sympathetic word, the loan anonymously given, the honest utterance even at a cost to oneself, the humility regarding one's accomplishments or attainments, these are all components of the life of righteousness. Or better, as our verses put it, they are all gates through which one may pass in order to come close to God.

How are they, however, one gate? What does it mean to say that they are all manifestations of a single theme or virtue, righteousness? What is their common denominator, beyond simply the name which we apply to them all? I would suggest that the common denominator is the recognition of and respect for the divine image in which the other has been created. Righteous behavior is that which testifies to the reality of this divine image. Righteous behavior, in all its forms, says yes to the reality of the divine image and to the infinite value which it entails. In that way it says yes to God.

The opportunity to serve God through righteous action toward one's fellow human beings is not experienced by the Psalmist as a burden, but rather as a cause for thanks. He seeks this path, the realization of which would stimulate in him further gratitude. He is grateful that he can live above the level of instinct. He is grateful that he can live a life of moral choice and action, that is, of moral dignity.

Finally, he sees this path as not a solitary one. Certainly, in acting righteously he must act toward other human beings. But he does not act alone. However much the moral level of society can be raised, there are already those who embody goodness and sacrifice and love. Perhaps they are not called by the name, "saints." But in their action, in what they do for those who cannot do for themselves, in the feeling of equality and fellow-humanity which they exude in a manner understated, they form a community which inspires and uplifts. The seeker is not alone. Community exists both as a goal and as a condition of his search.

In Leviticus 19:18, we read, "*Ve'ahavta le'reacha kamocha, Ani Adonai.*" "You shall love your neighbor as yourself, I am the Lord." It is through the love of one's neighbor that one may pass through the gate unto the Lord. Recognizing the dignity which this life and path entails, we give thanks also for the humility to which it, please God, awakens us. This is not the humility of nobodies, of mere "dust of the earth." This is the humility of those who may be servants of the Most

High. This humility is the quintessence of our dignity and for it we give thanks and express gratitude.

Gratitude, too, we feel toward those who inspire us with a vision of the life of righteousness, who reveal that in both the everyday and more urgent personal concerns of our fellow human beings we may—we must—become actively involved. A naughty little girl may also become a model who teaches and who leads. And a father who is exasperated may be relieved that the energy of his uncontrollable daughter can become the fuel for deeds of passionate caring and service. For the realness of possibility, for the dignity which is an opportunity ever-present, we say thank you to the source of both life and the transcendent dimension which shines within it. Thank you for the light which is radiated from souls who care and spirits who look beyond themselves.

THE HORSE AND THE HIDDEN SELF

In His original command to Abraham (at the time called, Abram), God says, "Go forth from your homeland and from the home of your father to the land that I will show you (Genesis 12:1)." God's purpose in sending Abraham forth is to enable the establishment of a new people, one through which all the peoples of the world shall become blessed.

The injunction to go forth, to leave the nest in which one was nurtured, reminds us of the fundamental characterization of man, following the creation of woman, in Genesis 2:24, "Therefore, a man shall depart from his father and his mother and cling to his wife, and they shall become one flesh." The need to separate is, of course, not that of the male alone, and I would suggest that this passage is best understood as applying to all human beings. We must all go forth, and through the discovery of a mate we may overcome, at least in part, the loneliness which is a fundamental possibility of human existence.

Separation is, thus, necessary, whether for the creation of a new national reality or for the creation of a new psychobiological reality, the twofold unity of a couple. In might be thought that the separation simply involves the movement away from or out of one's childhood framework so as to enable one to dwell within a new framework. In part, this is true. But this is not the whole truth.

The command to Abraham, I believe, suggests an element in the process of separation which is not grasped when we focus only on the transindividual reality which is born as a result of this process, or at least in part as a result of it. For the Hebrew words with which God begins His command are, "*lech lecha*," or as we have translated them, "go forth." These same words, however, may be taken to mean, "go unto yourself." Find yourself. Become yourself. Enable your self to blossom in the process of separation.

It is not being claimed that the self which one was within one's childhood family was not or could not be one's true self. It is being suggested, however, that the full unfolding of one's real self requires a movement beyond the familial framework of one's early years. Even in those societies in which many generations live together in one household the movement of the young into an adult stage of life involves their participation in a new family configuration. I, who was a son, am now a father. My father has thereby become a grandfather, and though we assume social roles identical to those who precede us, for us, in concrete life, there is newness. The familial structure abstracted by social scientists may be the same. But we are concrete people participating in it. We are concrete people living it. For each of us, for all of us together, there is newness. The individuality of each participant, as well as the individuality of each intergenerational family grouping, cannot be effaced. When I become an adult, I am, indeed, beyond the familial framework of my early years.

Why does the Torah, with its emphasis upon family, state, on our reading, that one must "go unto oneself?" As the verse in Genesis suggests, we are in need of others. We are in need of a felt connection with others. A person is not, by nature, an isolate. And yet, in one's relations to others it is possible to lose oneself. There need be no overt pressure on the part of others that one do so. There need be no will, conscious or unconscious, to violate the integrity or authenticity of another. But the larger social reality within which one finds oneself may interfere with, as well as nurture, the unfolding of the self within. If others, through no fault of their own, are excessively blocked in their ability to make contact, simple, direct emotional contact with another, then that other may become turned inward in order to defend and protect himself.

To not be met as the self one actually is, to not be met as one's natural or original self, is to experience the rejection of that self. I do not say that that self has been actively rejected. I do not say that there is a will to reject that self. But the self, in not being socially confirmed, experiences itself as rejected. Even if one remains outwardly energetic in manner, even if one seems vitally alive, this aliveness is not fueled by one's real self and is, therefore, not authentic or is only partially authentic. In the extreme case there may be a forgetfulness of the real self. The person may no longer be consciously aware of the fact that the self he is living is not himself. Have you ever met a person who had become, in effect, a mask and you could not deduce who was there behind the mask? Have you ever met a person who had become a mask and were not sure if that person was aware that he was living a mask?

The story is told of a student who came running frantically into the office of the American philosopher, Morris Raphael Cohen. He told Cohen that he was not sure if he had a self. What could Cohen say to him? Cohen said that he would be happy to provide the young person with an answer, if he would only tell him to whom he should address it.

If in this story, no doubt apocryphal, Cohen had really given such an answer, he would have been guilty of cruel insensitivity. The student was not asking an abstract question about whether or not he had a self. He was suffering from an identity crisis. He did not know who he was. But that, I would suggest, is already a measure of real progress beyond the case of the person who has become a mask. He does not know who his real self is. But he does not know that he does not know. He is lost in forgetfulness. He is asleep, and asleep to the fact that he is asleep. Cohen's student has awoken, though in a state of anxiety. His anxiety is testimony to the possibility of his becoming the self he truly is, a possibility he is now challenged to realize.

Sometimes a more palpable sign than the student's anxiety may remain, indicating that a person has departed from his true self. This sign may not even be recognized as such, but may be maintained as a reminder, only unconsciously understood, of who that self is. In its being maintained the possibility is also preserved that the true self will one day awaken into consciousness, no longer fearful of rejection. Strengthened by his own self-acceptance and self-affirmation, he discovers that social reality, while short of Messianic perfection, is not as threatening and rejecting as he had believed.

Some years ago, when I lived in Ann Arbor, Michigan, I became friends with a young man who was studying to be a social worker. As part of the preparation for work in his field, he had to engage in the supervised treatment of psychiatric patients. He told me of a case in which a patient had carried with him for many years the memory of a picture which he had drawn in nursery school. Only a handful of memories remained from those early years, and this is one that had stuck with him. As he thought back, he recalled that the picture, which was of a horse, had been considered very beautiful by his teacher. In fact, she considered it so beautiful that she called over

Davin Wolok

another teacher to see it. But he, though cognizant of the presence of the teachers admiring his picture, did not really pay any attention to them. He simply gazed at the picture. Aware that it was well done, he was drawn by something other than its aesthetic quality. The question of a hidden meaning in the picture did not become formulated in his mind, and so he made no effort to grasp what it might be. But the memory of the picture and of his gazing upon it remained.

Years later, while in therapy, he felt pressed to try to understand what had been a "sleeping question" until that time. In speaking with another therapist he was offered an interpretation of the picture which somehow did not resonate with him. And when he saw my friend, he spoke of that earlier frustrated effort to gain understanding. Rather than provide an explanation of his own, my friend simply asked him what he thought the picture meant. Suddenly, with tears streaming down his face, the man said that the horse was himself. It represented him in his true aliveness. But this real self had, as it were, become "papermachied" over, so as to present a self to his family which would be accepted. It was not that in his outward traits he had become someone entirely different from who he would have been otherwise. But in key respects, not fully compatible with himself, he had identified with the feelings and attitudes of others simply in order to gain their approval. With his real self not met in a natural, direct way, with this real self not emotionally validated, he had assumed an identity which would make him acceptable. Finally, in the presence of my friend he came to a recognition of the presence of his real self, who had never fully given up the battle and who had, after maintaining himself in secret, finally begun the push out toward self-liberation. Therapy continued and self-acceptance was coupled with a growing recognition of the legitimacy and worthiness of his real self in the eyes of others. Understanding of those from whom he had not received the nurturance for which he had yearned as a child gradually developed, and with this love, as well, began to bud.

Hermann Hesse, in the prologue to his novel, *Demian*, writes that

> Each man's life represents a road toward himself, an attempt at such a road, the intimation of a path. No man has ever been entirely and completely himself. Yet each one

strives to become that—one in an awkward, the other in a more intelligent way, each as best he can.... each of us—experiments of the depths—strives toward his own destiny.

Not all of us will achieve the originality of selfhood of Abraham. God willing, most will be saved from the life of a mask who is unaware of the loss of his real self. But may we all attempt to heed the injunction, "Go unto yourself." May we all strive to listen to the voice which whispers to us from within, whether in picture or symbol, whether in memory or fantasy. May we all become the self we were created to be and, in so doing, enlarge our capacity to validate the selfhood of others. In the authenticity of meeting is true selfhood born.

STRUGGLES OF A SON
A Second Case of "Traditional" Parshanut

One night a young man flies into a rage. He enters the family shop and begins to smash the merchandise, undermining his father's ability to earn a living and humiliating him before the community. "What happened to this fine young fellow?," people wonder. "He was so intelligent, so responsible, so helpful to his Dad prior to this episode of madness."

The father, on the morning following, confronts the son concerning the meaning of his rampage. "How could you do this? Have I ever treated you with disrespect? Do you know what this means to the family?," he asks. The son responds, "You are a fake. Your merchandise is worthless. You act as if it will bring your customers some benefit. But it's all a deception. I finally realized this and did what I had to do."

The father, amazingly, does not react with hurt at this attack upon his character. He asks further what the son might be referring to. The son goes on, "You sell sculptures which you claim are something more than mere human artifacts. You tell the people they will bring them health and prosperity and long life. You speak of your sculptures as if they are gods and, in fact, say that they are."

Of whom are we speaking in this vignette? Who are the father and son who confront each other across an abyss of contrary understandings and conflicting perspectives? While I have made certain alterations in the traditional Midrash, or imaginative rabbinic embellishment upon the Biblical tale, giving its hero more the cast of a sixties rebel, I am speaking, in fact, of our ancestor Abraham (then called Abram) and his father Terah.

Terah, we are told, was a seller of idols. And Abraham one night took it upon himself to destroy his father's idols, so as to expose their emptiness as divine figures. When his father beheld the broken idols, Abraham told him that they had been fighting. From their own battle arose the scattered fragments. Terah, of course, realized that idols cannot fight, or engage in any other action, and from this Abraham was able to show that they were not gods, but mere, lifeless artifacts.

Abraham, through whom we learn that God is a singular spiritual being transcending the physical world, was, thus, not only his father's challenger, but his educator, as well.

Now I do not want to suggest that Terah was a monotheist and no advance in spiritual consciousness was achieved through his son Abraham. But the Biblical account, though spare, is actually richer than the conventional understanding, revealing a kinship between Terah and Abraham which goes beyond the biological. The two are together, if you wish, a two-stage rocket in which the first stage, Terah, can only get so far in the effort to transcend his roots, while the second stage, Abraham, nourished by a family environment open to movement and change, is finally able to fly free, entering a new spiritual orbit, revolutionary in character and eternal in its impact and significance.

The relations between generations, the relation between relations, is a theme which permeates our few brief verses about Abraham and Terah, beginning in Genesis 11:24 and continuing through the opening verses of Genesis 12. In exploring these relations and the milieu from which Abraham arose, in probing the complexity which characterized his soul, perhaps we will discover something about ourselves, children of an iconoclast who did not simply "split from home," but rather "lifted off" from a "launching pad" which his less radical father had prepared.

To begin with, let us note that, contrary to popular belief, when Abraham ultimately receives the command to leave his homeland, it is not in Ur Kasdim, his hometown, that he receives the command. For Terah and Abraham and Sarah (then called Sarai) and Abraham's nephew Lot have already left Ur, setting off for the land of Canaan. More precisely, as Genesis 11:31 points out, Terah takes Abraham and Sarah and Lot (who is a grandson, the son of his own deceased son Haran), initiating their collective journey to Canaan. Before reaching their destination, however, they stop and settle in Charan, a city whose name has an interesting aural affinity to the name of the departed Haran. Could Terah get no further? Was he psychologically impeded from fully leaving behind his homeland Mesopotamia, where he had buried his son?

The themes of independence and interconnectedness have already manifested themselves in the life of Terah. In Genesis 11:26 we read that he fathered three sons, Abraham (or again, Abram), Nahor and Haran, and the wording already indicates that Terah was a substantial figure in his own right. For it begins, "Now this is the family line of Terah: Terah begot Abram, Nahor and Haran..." Contrast this with Genesis 25:29, describing Isaac: "Now this is the family line of Isaac, son of Abraham; Abraham begot Isaac." Here the individual upon whom we focus has his identity only through his father. He is "Isaac, son of Abraham." And in case we don't get the point, the verse adds, "Abraham begot Isaac." In Genesis 11:26 we read of Terah, not of "Terah, son of Nahor." And we learn of what he did, namely, that he begot three sons, not that he was begotten by his father. Terah was a somebody, one who moreover could venture out from his hometown on a journey, even if uncompleted, toward a new land.

At the same time, Terah did not simply cut himself off from his past, as we can see when we examine the names of his children—or at least one of his children. Terah's own father was Nahor. And when Terah's first son Abraham, was born, the father did not experience a special need to preserve his own father's name. Was Nahor still alive? Or had he perhaps already died, but a sense of permanent loss did not fully set in? Whatever the answer, by the time his second son is born Terah experiences a clear need to memorialize his father and names this son Nahor after him. Terah combines within the independence of one who is willing to depart for a new land, with the filial piety of one who never forgets his familial roots.

Now what about Abraham? Until he receives the command in Genesis 12:1 to leave his homeland, he apparently had no intention of completing the journey to Canaan. But when does he have the inner readiness to go? When does God find him in a state of spiritual openness to break out fully from the cultural framework of Mesopotamia in which he had grown up? The answer, as we read in Genesis 11:32, is only after Terah himself has passed on. Abraham would not abandon his father, who never overcame his grief at the premature death of his son Haran. But Abraham was not one to stay put even in the absence of an overarching moral obligation. When this no longer existed, the stage was set for a new phase in the process which had already begun in Ur.

It is no overstatement to speak of the process as one of liberation, of spiritual-cultural liberation, when the language of the text is closely examined. I am not suggesting that the participants were aware of the ultimate significance of their travels, as preparatory for a new spiritual adventure. Nor am I intimating that God had directed His attention to any but Abraham as an agent-to-be for his project-in-the-making. But that there was a higher meaning to the journey from Ur is implied by the language in Genesis 11:31, when we read concerning Terah, Abraham, Sarah and Lot, "*vayeitzu itam me-Ur Kasdim,*" "and they went out together from Ur Kasdim." The verb, "*vayeitzu,*" coming from the Hebrew root, "*yatzo,*" is rich in associations. For this is the same root which is used later in Genesis 15:7, when God says to Abraham, "*Ani Adonai asher hotzeiticha me'Ur Kasdim,*" "I am the Lord who took you out of Ur Kasdim," the verb, "*hotzeiticha,*" deriving from "*yatzo.*" Finally, this latter passage inevitably calls to mind the first of the Ten Commandments, which reads, "*Anochi Adonai Elohecha asher hotzeiticha me'Eretz Mitzrayim, mibeit avadim,*" "I am the Lord, your God, who took you out of the land of Egypt, the house of bondage." Leaving Ur Kasdim is kindred to leaving Egypt! Leaving Ur Kasdim is an exodus from bondage to a false vision and a delusive way of life!

Leaving Mesopotamia entirely is the phase when the second stage of the rocket, the Abrahamic stage, is finally liberated into a new orbit, which shall begin to germinate in Canaan. For the culture of Mesopotamia was a powerful and attractive one. Even with the support of his courageous wife Sarah, departing was no easy task. Still Abraham, nurtured by the restlessness and mobility in the household of his father Terah, was the unique individual up to the task not only of setting off—but of beginning. It was to him that God could give the charge and promise of being the father of a new nation, one with redemptive and liberationist implications for all humanity. "For all the families of the earth shall be blessed through you," we read in Genesis 12:3. From this unto the proclamation, "Nation shall not lift up sword unto nation, neither shall they learn war anymore," in Isaiah 2:4, there is one but spiritual breath, which animates and vivifies a people both open to and uneasy with the mission which has become its destiny.

Who is this man Abraham, not simply a rejector of his past, but the courageous agent of a vision soaring beyond all that his father could imagine or grasp? Who is this man Abraham, from whom we

144

learn that the future is not simply a repetition of the past, but a path enabling the realization of possibilities, a path where hope finds its ultimate confirmation?

Abraham is, indeed, the sign of a new creation even in the midst of a world already created.

Abraham is the one who testifies to God by walking on—alone.

FROM THE FRYING PAN INTO THE FIRE OF — REDEMPTION

During my teenage years I became acquainted with an approach to scripture known as Biblical criticism. This did not occur in any Hebrew high school class, though the religious philosophy of the synagogue where the school was located was not incompatible with this approach. My acquaintance with Biblical criticism was made through my happening upon a book which purported to refute it.

While I cannot recall the circumstances in which I came upon this book, I would assume, in retrospect, that my discovery of it was not entirely accidental. I must have been reflecting upon questions concerning the origin and validity of our faith, and out of an earnest desire to quiet any unsettling thoughts, turned to a work which aimed to shore up the traditional view of things.

As I say, my synagogue's religious philosophy was not incompatible with Biblical criticism. But this approach was not taught in the school, and I would suspect that, even with the adult members of our congregation, it was discussed seldom. The traditional view, that the Torah in its entirety was revealed at Mt. Sinai, is the one with which most synagogue-goers were familiar. True, the text may not at times have seemed quite as unified as one would expect, given that view. A mere singing of the Friday evening hymn, "Lecha Dodi," would remind one of a difference in wording between two versions of the Ten Commandments, one from the Book of Exodus and the other from the Book of Deuteronomy. And the hymn's assertion that God spoke these two versions simultaneously might not readily convince. Such reflections, however, were rarely, if ever, entertained in a focused and explicit fashion. The Torah was still typically described as a unified text, arising in a single miraculous moment in history.

Bible critics claim that the Torah is neither a perfect unity nor an all-at-once creation. Rather, it is a synthesis of sources from different times, reflecting different outlooks. One must look for the human group or situation out of which a source arose. Even if one maintains a religious, though non-Orthodox, approach and claims that God spoke through different people in different circumstances,

146

the fact remains that in the eyes of Biblical criticism the Torah is not a seamless whole. There are divergent emphases in different portions of the Torah. There are contradictions in content. There is, at most, for the non-Orthodox religious, a human hand, or rather a multitude of human hands, through which the divine voice transcribes. That this divine voice lies behind the multiplicity of human authors is itself an act of faith. For the divergent backgrounds and differing perspectives of the authors are what is emphasized. It is not simply, for example, that the same God at times presents Himself as an august, transcendent being and at others as an intimate presence. It is rather that authors of different backgrounds saw God in these differing ways. Their situations in life and perspectives are what count. If in the traditional approach we begin with God turning toward people and addressing them, here we focus on human attitudes toward the divine. If as traditionalists we speak of revelation, as critics we speak of religious philosophy.

Some time ago I wondered if the approach of Biblical criticism could be presented in a lighter, "less hifalutin" way. That is, could we look behind the stories of the Torah and find ordinary situations which would make sense to the "average" person? The story of Jacob's wrestling with the angel was the first that came to mind. At the conclusion of this story we read, "*Vayizrach lo hashemesh ka'asher avar et Penuel vehu tzolea al yereicho*," "And the sun shone upon him as he passed by Penuel, and he was limping on his thigh (Genesis 32:31)." Now the Torah attributes the impairment of Jacob's thigh, and his consequent difficulty in walking, to a dislocation incurred in the process of wrestling. He bested an angel, but did not come out unscathed.

Reading this story I came up with a different explanation for Jacob's limp. Some may call it Midrashic. I call it "natural insight." Jacob, as you know, had two wives, Rachel and Leah. Rachel he really loved, having worked for fourteen years until he was allowed to marry her. But Leah he was tricked into marrying. He wasn't too nuts about her. In fact, he felt that both he and she would be better off if she were back in her hometown, Haran. Leah was not oblivious to Jacob's feelings, and at times her anger and frustration got the best of her. One day, when Jacob was bugging her in the kitchen about what she was preparing for dinner, Leah told him to leave her alone. Jacob could see that he was "getting Leah's goat" and wouldn't let up on his annoying patter. Finally, Leah had enough, and she picked up a frying pan, ran toward Jacob and gave him one good whack on the thigh! Boy did Jacob hurt. But his embarrassment was even greater. What would he tell his buddies when they saw him hobbling along the next day? That he, forefather of a great nation-to-be, could not even keep order in his own family? That he was not master in his own house? Jacob decided to cook up a story which would save him from the title of henpecked husband. He would say that he had gotten into a fight with an angel, and while he came out on top, he had twisted his thigh. In no time he would be back to normal.

Now if we wish to find other stories which contain the motif of the man who has suffered a physical impairment, and perhaps identify them with a single source, we have not far to look. In fact, we need but turn to the beginning of the Torah, where we read of a rib being removed from Adam for the creation of Eve. (True, she wasn't yet named in this story... but we know who she is.) What could really account for this story? The following, I would suggest.

Adam was a very shy individual. He wanted to develop a relationship with a woman, but was afraid to do so. He tried to cover this up by presenting himself as a self-sufficient male. Finally, one day he got up the courage to show an interest in a woman, but was embarrassed to admit that he needed another human being. What would he say when seen with his new friend? (If you say there was no one else around, just remember that not everyone is mentioned in the Torah. Who, for example, was Cain afraid of when he was exiled from his home? In terms of what's written, there were no other people besides Adam and Even and his slain brother, Abel.) Now Adam couldn't deny that Eve existed, and his lack of complete emotional independence would have to be acknowledged. So, Adam tried to minimize the "damage" by portraying his friend as in a profound sense dependent on him. Why, she was, in fact, created out of his very own body. He was the one chosen by God for the first "cloning operation." After he was anesthetized, a rib was removed from him and transformed into a female companion. He was, so to speak, expanded into two people. He wasn't needy. He was made larger. He, a male, was amazingly enough, a mother!

Now I don't propose the above interpretations with utter

seriousness, but do believe that when we approach the stories of the Torah we should see not only outward events, but struggles having to do with identity and relationship and change. In the story of Adam the need of a human being for a mate or companion is clearly expressed. And the story of Jacob is one in which our patriarch advanced from one level of selfhood to another. His struggle with a higher dimension of reality, an "angel," if you will, now became part and parcel of his understanding of who he was. More precisely, it became part and parcel of the reality of who he was. As a young man, fleeing his brother, Esau, Jacob issued a number of requests to God, stating that if they were fulfilled, he would be loyal to the Almighty. Now he even more forcefully asserts himself, but recognizes the independent reality and significance of the divine claim upon him. God is present as the one to whom he must respond, and with whom he may even have to contend, and the tension between himself as a human being and God as his commanding other has become and shall continue to be part of his very identity. Thus, he is given the new name, "Israel," or "the one who struggles with God."

Why, emerging from the battle with the angel, does Jacob limp? Does this not indicate a falling back, rather than a moving forward? The Torah, I believe, presents a non-simplistic approach to the process of growth. Growth is not easy. Advancing to a new level of being may involve meeting head on the "slings and arrows" which life hurls against us. We may find our most central convictions challenged. We may be disappointed by those in whom we had the greatest confidence. We may discover that we had illusions not only about others, but about ourselves, and can no longer maintain the inflated self-conception of our earlier years. But all this need not lead to self-condemnation or cynicism. When we have lost our naive certainty, the world may appear richer and more mysterious. When we have ceased to demand perfection of others, we may find that there is goodness in them, too. And when we have relinquished the requirement that we be without blemish, we may realize the value in our lives and our meaning to family and friends and even acquaintances.

In comparison with our image of ourselves as "Olympics runners," it will appear that we now limp. And, indeed, there will be some truth in this. But miraculously enough, it is with this newborn consciousness that we will have ascended to a higher level in our self-awareness and comportment toward others. We will have become more humble, and we will have grown. Freed of the childlike faith in a God with whom evil and absurdity cannot coexist, we may now discover that a trust in God may be mixed with perplexity concerning much that occurs in the world. We may question—and will question—how innocent suffering can be permitted. We may doubt, return to faith, doubt again, and return once more. We will "wrestle with God," sometimes every inch of the way. We will be children of Jacob, or more precisely, children of Israel.

Still the Bible claims, this is not the end of the story. And here a feature of scripture which was long underappreciated by Bible critics will illumine the way. For with contradiction between different Biblical texts, there is also interconnectedness. One verse, separated even by a multitude of books from another, may be a response to that latter verse. In our instance I am thinking of the words which begin chapter 3, verse 20 of the Book of Malachi, the final prophet of ancient Israel. There we read, *"Vezarcha lachem yirei sh'mi shemesh tzedakah umarpei bichnafeha,"* "But unto you who revere My name a sun of righteousness shall shine, with healing in her wings..." Jacob, our ancestor, started life intact. But in advancing to a higher level of existence he began to "limp." Now those of his descendants who persevere in a true relationship with God shall overcome the stage of "limping." They shall be healed by the light which comes from "a sun of righteousness." No longer shall the idolatrous worship of power and money and status and fame have the dominance which it currently enjoys in life. No longer shall false gods, all founded upon a hyperconcern with the ego, be the deities which humans serve. The freedom which derives from fellowship shall be the healing which comes to those who have transcended their egos. More precisely, they have transcended their egos, while standing their ground as their own true selves.

The term, "religion," originally means, "to be bound back." This suggests that the goal we are to seek is not one which is alien from our own being. Sent out from our mother's womb, from, as it were, the "Garden of Eden" of our biological existence, we become more and more individuated as egos. We each attempt to create a viable self who can wend his or her way in the world. But the temptation is present, and may even be socially endorsed, to exalt the self. To the degree that this is succumbed to, the ability to taste spiritual fulfillment is diminished. For one is focused on that which is finite and mortal, namely, one's own self, and from such a foundation no sense of eternal meaning can be firmly established. In our prayers we say, "Return us to You, O God," because we wish to reinstill in ourselves the consciousness of a spiritual link which is there from the beginning. The process which Jacob began and which Malachi described in its consummation is one in which we arrive at the living awareness of a tie to God and to godly values which is not new, but renewed.

However many hands were involved in composing the Torah, however many sources may lie behind the Bible, this process, through struggle to righteousness, through life to return, is one which pulsates in the words of sacred scripture. No. Jacob did not limp from being struck in the kitchen. And he did not, while fleeing a frying pan, leap into a fire. From the light of a spiritual sun, from the radiance of godly lives and the divine presence, will healing, God willing, come to his descendants, whose hope is for redemption and the full realization of a tie which never grows old.

Part III

*FROM THE BIG BANG TO MY
ZEIDA DOVID TZVI:
SERMONS FOR TODAY—AND HOPEFULLY
TOMORROW*

*"The Virtues of Seeing, and Seeing—That We See Not":
A Sermon on Parshat Toldot*
*"Toward the Day of Our Longing": A Sermon on Parshat
Vayehi*
"I Have, Indeed, Appeared!": A Sermon on Parshat Vaera
"From Slavery to Light": A Sermon on Parshat Bo
"From the Scene at Sinai": A Sermon on Parshat Yitro
"Faith in the Journey": A Sermon on Parshat Masei
"A Parshah of Words": A Sermon on Parshat Devarim
*"For Life and Eternity are Joined Each into the Other":
A Sermon in Response to Parshat Ki Tetzei*
"Beyond the Chains of Illusion": A Sermon for Passover
"Fearful Freedom": A Sermon for Passover
"For Love is Stronger Than Death!": A Yizkor Sermon

THE VIRTUES OF SEEING, AND SEEING—
THAT WE SEE NOT
A Sermon on Parshat Toldot

In today's Parshah, Toldot, we read, "*Vayehi ki zakein Yitzchak vatichhena einav meiriot,*" "And it occurred when Isaac was old that his eyes grew dim from seeing," or in other words, that he became blind. It was in this condition that he sent out and awaited his son, Esau, to whom he believed he would give the blessing of the first-born. As it well known, the second-born son, Jacob, shows up wearing hairy skins on his arms, convincing his father that he is really Esau, thus receiving the blessing which was presumably his brother's due. Isaac does recognize that Jacob sounds exactly like Jacob, but is convinced through the ruse of the hairy skins that Jacob is Esau. Because of his blindness, Isaac is deceived.

Or is he? The interpretation has been advanced that at least on some subconscious level Isaac knew to whom he was speaking. After all, can the evidence of an identifiable voice be so easily discarded? According to this interpretation, Isaac realized, at least on some level, that Jacob was the more suitable son to receive the chief blessing. He would be the more appropriate transmitter of the faith and vision of his father, Abraham, and thus was, in effect, willingly deceived by Jacob. In his own way, he was in on the ruse which his wife and Jacob's mother, Rebecca, had devised. His blindness, if you wish, served as his excuse.

It is my intent today to focus on the whole question of seeing and not seeing. What is the nature of each? Does seeing involve more than simply picking up visual stimuli from the environment? May not seeing, or at least the recognition that we do not always see, have a positive meaning? Do we have something important to learn from the blind? Is there any sense in which we are all blind?

Let me begin by pointing out that in the eyes of the Siddur, or Jewish prayerbook, we are all originally blind. We start each day by being blind, but then with the help of God may achieve vision. As the fifth of the Birkot Hashachar, or Morning Benedictions, reads, "*Baruch Atah Adonai, Eloheinu Melech HaOlam, Pokeiach Ivrim,*"

"Blessed are You, O Lord our God, King of the universe, Who gives sight to the blind." Who is being spoken of here? Clearly, it is not people who are conventionally blind. The Birkot Hashachar, or Morning Benedictions, are recited by everybody — and in relation to everybody. When I recite this blessing, I am speaking of myself as a blind person, who is being given sight. It is, thus, regarded as possible for a person who has no physical impairment in relation to seeing to not see. Such not seeing may involve not picking up what is right before one, even though there is nothing wrong with one's eyes. It may also involve not seeing things for what they are, being deceived by appearances, even though one picks up the visual stimuli.

A simple example of the former occurred to me when I was a child. I was looking for a jar of mustard in the refrigerator and could not find it. Finally, I found it when I realized that I was staring right at it. I have never forgotten that experience. It did not involve a major discovery. It resulted in no major insight. It was just the unforgettable experience of looking directly at something and not grasping its presence. Everything was right for me to see. But I did not see.

In the story of Abraham's concubine, Hagar, and her son, Ishamel, the Torah presents such an instance of something being apparent and yet not seen. Hagar is overcome by worry that her son, Ishmael, will die for want of water. She is at wits end and does not know what to do. Finally, the Torah writes, God opened her eyes and she saw a well of water nearby. Why did she not see it before? It was because her anxiety drowned out her full consciousness of the environment. The answer was there. But she could not see it.

Sometimes a terrible trauma can cause vision to be impaired. In fact, the trauma might not even have its effect immediately. Yet, when it occurs, it is clear that the trauma was the cause. Torah scholar, Aviva Zornberg, writes in her book, *Genesis: The Beginning of Desire*, of the blindness "afflicting women survivors of the Cambodian massacres. A considerable time after the Khmer Rouge horrors, and after they had found refuge in the United States, women began to complain of eyesight problems. No organic disorder was diagnosed, and existing diagnostic categories... did not entirely fit. What the women had seen, years before, had made it necessary to suppress vision, to repress emotional response." In this instance it was not the horror of what loomed, or was believed to loom, as with Hagar, but the horror of what had been actually seen which triggered, though in a delayed manner, the reaction of impaired vision.

It might be believed that the same was actually the case with Isaac. Perhaps the sight of his father holding a knife over him, when he was bound to the altar to be sacrificed, caused the blindness of his later years. Recall that the Torah speaks of Isaac's eyes growing dim "from seeing." Perhaps he saw too much, or what he saw was too terrifying. And finally he could see no more.

But the cases of Hagar and the Cambodian women and Isaac are not the normal cases. They are not the reason that the Siddur speaks of us as blind. I would suggest that it is for lesser reasons that we sometimes do not see. Seeing makes us uncomfortable. We like our illusions. We like the good feeling it gives us—or at least superficially gives us. In a chapter entitled, "The President's Speech," from his book, *The Man Who Mistook His Wife For A Hat*, Oliver Sacks, a world-renowned neurologist, writes, "*What* was going on? A roar of laughter was coming from the aphasia ward, just as the President's speech was coming on, and they had all been so eager to hear the President speaking...

There he was, the old Charmer, the Actor, with his practised rhetoric, his histrionisms, his emotional appeal—and all the patients were convulsed with laughter. Well, not all: some looked bewildered, some looked outraged, one or two looked apprehensive, but most looked amused. The President was, as always, moving—but he was moving them, apparently, mainly to laughter. What could they be thinking? Were they failing to understand him? Or did they, perhaps understand him all too well?

It was often said of these patients, who though intelligent had the severest receptive or global aphasia, rendering them incapable of understanding words as such, that they none the less understood most of what was said to them." As Sacks writes of the aphasiac, "He cannot grasp your words, and so cannot be deceived by them; but what he grasps he grasps with infallible precision, namely the *expression* that goes with the words, that total, spontaneous, involuntary expressiveness which can never be simulated or faked, as words alone can, all too easily..." He continues, "to any falsity or impropriety in bodily appearance or posture, aphasiacs are preternaturally sensitive. And if they cannot see one—this is especially true of our blind aphasiacs—they have an infallible ear for every vocal nuance, the tone, the rhythm, the candences, the music, the subtlest modulations, inflections, intonations, which can give—or remove—versimilitude to or from a man's voice.

In this, then, lies their power of understanding—understanding without words, what is authentic or inauthentic. Thus it was the grimaces, the histrionisms, the false gestures and, above all, the false tones and cadences of the voice, which rang false for these wordless but immensely sensitive patients. It was to these (for them) most flaring, even grotesque, incongruities and improprieties that my aphasic patients responded, undeceived and undeceivable by words.

This is why they laughed at the President's speech."

As Sacks writes, "Here then was the paradox of the President's speech. We normals—aided, doubtless, by our wish to be fooled, were indeed well and truly fooled..."

So, there you have it. Seeing is not simply the result of picking up visual stimuli from the environment. Seeing results from reading the stimuli correctly, or first and foremost, from being willing to.

In the case just presented the unappealing characteristics of a person or of his behavior were not attended to. But sometimes we block out the immensely positive because we perceive the other through a limiting and distorting framework. I am grateful for the liberating effect of morally enlightened teachings, which enabled me to experience in a striking way this last year that more which a person may bring when seen first and foremost simply as a person. I should add that morally enlightened teachings may beget the kind of treatment from others which enables people suffering from limiting conditions to open up and reveal more freely that more which they have and are.

My wife, Carol, and I were visiting our daughter, Rina, at Beaver Run, a residential school for the developmentally disabled where she was working. We were sitting in the living room of the house where the children in her care lived, with our shoes off, a practice followed to prevent mud from being tracked in. A girl I shall call Margaret would come and plop herself down between Carol and me on the couch, smiling as she played with our hands. Margaret had a special fascination with both hands and feet, and on one occasion she came in and picked up my right foot, holding it by the big toe. I wouldn't say that Margaret gave me a deep, penetrating look. She kind of gazed, but right at me, and it was clear that she was trying to make direct person-to-person contact. I felt uplifted, even redeemed.

Margaret was in her way making what the philosopher, Martin Buber, calls I-Thou contact between people. Here she was, a severely disabled child, who was moreover deaf and mute, but clearly she was more than her condition, or host of conditions. She was, as the school emphasized, a soul, who was deeper and greater than any condition. In view of how she would still be seen by some members of our society, I should also add that Margaret was African-American. I will never forget her or what she means to me.

Nor will I ever forget another child, now an adult, who taught me that the power of one's presence and participation in the visible world does not depend on one's capacity to see it. Meaningfully apprehending one's environment and impacting on it depends more on the vision in one's mind and soul. I am thinking back to my experience here at Mishkan Tefila of teaching Tasha Chemel, who was at the time a Bat Mitzvah student. I have always felt that my greatest moment with Tasha was when I was taping some material for her and suddenly my voice cracked. Tasha burst out laughing and could not contain herself. She just kept laughing and laughing. I felt so good. Here was a blind girl, who felt totally confident and secure and could relax and just let go in the same environment I inhabited. In fact, her comfort in the visible world was so great that at times I literally forgot that she was blind. When Tasha gave the speech preceding the Haftarah at her Bat Mitzvah, she spoke with the conviction and poise of an experienced orator and her voice rang out across the sanctuary. What she lacked in physical sight she more than made up for in intellectual and spiritual insight. Sometimes, you know, when we see, we don't see, and when we don't see, we do. Only in a state of blindness did Shakespeare's King Lear finally come to perceive accurately who was sincere and who was not, who was true and loving and who was a murderous charlatan.

Is there an eye of the soul? Can we sense what is present even when we cannot grasp the visual detail? Helen Keller writes, "People sometimes seem surprised that I love the ocean when I cannot see it. But I do not think it is strange. It is because God has planted the love of His wonderful works deep in the hearts of His children, and whether we see them or not, we feel everywhere their beauty and mystery

You Can Come Home Again

enfolding us." I should tell you that on Simchat Torah, when I have read the story of creation at the beginning of Genesis, I have, even though not seeing them, felt Rabbi Pritzker's and Cantor Finklestein's presence at they stood by this lectern. The power and majesty of this passage obviously awoke in them a heightened state of soul presence, which could be felt even when they were not visually perceived.

Who truly sees and who does not? Some people see part of the truth or at least how things appear within one perspective and believe it to be the whole truth. Others, among them the greatest minds of the human race, place an emphasis on the limits of human knowledge. Neither arrogance nor despair accompanies their attaining of human understanding, but humility and a sense of participating in a wider and richer, though mysterious, reality. Thus, Socrates, for example, said, "The only thing I know is that I don't know." Woody Allen, thinking that even this was too much, retorted, "Well then how do you know that?"

In considering the question of seeing and not seeing, we are brought to reflect on central values of human life. First, we learn that without courage we shall never see. We might wish to be deceived, but our lives will grow fuller and truer if we dispense with the comfort that comes from letting ourselves be deceived. Second, we learn the value of gratitude. For even by those who we might think lack the capacity to make an impact we may be touched in a deep and life-long way. We might encounter those without physical sight as, to use the Talmud's term, *Sagi Nahor*, or filled with light, both in their capacity to fill our world with light and in their capacity to teach us how to see even when we pick up no visual stimuli. Finally, we might learn the value of humility, for all of us, as both the Siddur and intellectual greats have seen, are in large measure *ivrim*, or blind. When we accept that fact, however, we need not feel despair. Rather we might experience wonderment at a world whose mysteries we can never fully understand.

To be aware of our true state, as seeing and not seeing, and to value both modalities, we will return to our true selves, freed of the need to know and control all, free to experience life and the wonders of the world with the openness and flexibility of children, though now with an adult consciousness.

Blessed are You, O Lord, our God, King of the universe, who more than sight, gives us insight, if we but allow You to do so.

TOWARD THE DAY OF OUR LONGING
A Sermon on Parshat Vayehi

Fifteen billion years ago a bomb went off. This bomb was so small that if a human being had been around, he would not have been able to see it. But this bomb, when it exploded, created a fireball so intense that it expanded and expanded, literally creating out of its midst the chemical elements from which the material bodies of the universe are formed. It spawned planets and stars and comets and meteors and galaxies. It gave birth to all that was and is and will be in the physical universe. And in the midst of its furious and mindless productivity it brought forth a planet so modest in size that it would appear to be but a speck if seen from a distance very short by cosmic standards. From a bit further, it would not be seen at all.

Millions of years passed and one day, through a process not yet understood, the first spark of life came into existence on this planet. From this life new life came, and through an accidental series of events, one species after another evolved. Species came and species went. Those blessed with luck survived. And finally, through a journey governed by chance, a new life-form appeared that asked what this mysterious, perplexing, wondrous and amazing world was all about. How did it get here? How did they, the bearers of these questions, get here? The answer, the true answer, was that it had all occurred without rhyme or reason. The repeating patterns of nature, the alteration of day and night, the procession of the seasons, the cycle of an individual's life, the succession of the generations, had all come into being without any intention, without any mind or will behind them. A bomb had exploded. An accidental evolution of life-forms had transpired. The world was truly a tale told by an idiot. Such is the case not if what science teaches us is truth, but if it is the whole truth.

Today we have read Parshat Vayehi, thereby completing the Book of Genesis, a work in which the Biblical vision first begins to unfold. Customarily, efforts have been made to show that there is no conflict between this great religious document and science by starting from the belief that science teaches us the facts. Here's what happened.

Here's how the world works. You can believe whatever you want in addition, for example, that there is a God, as long as you accept what science asserts. You can believe, if you wish, in the Biblical tale of creation as long as you explain the six days of creation as really six periods of immense duration. The conflict between science and religion is overcome by adjusting religion to science.

Now what I believe is not that we should reject scientific accounts of the history of the world, but that the Biblical vision, first laid out in Genesis, goes beyond what science teaches. Its view is the larger one, the more encompassing one. It presents the big picture, one in which the world has meaning—and we have meaning. Prior to seeing how that meaning comes to be expressed in Parshat Vayehi, let me make some general comments concerning it.

As with science, Genesis, and the Bible as a whole, says that the world has an order. There are repeating patterns and cycles of nature. And even when things occur which are surprising or unexpected— New England weather is a good example of that—still the world is not a raging chaos. Science, it should be noted, while speaking of the accidental nature of evolution, still believes that things can't happen in any which-way. From a cow you will not get an elephant. From a parakeet you will not get a giraffe.

But here's where we get to the crucial dividing point, the point we begin to learn in Genesis, and which comes to its crystallization in Parshat Vayehi. That is that in addition to the repeating patterns of nature, which for the Bible exist because an intelligent Creator put them there, there is an overall goal toward which the world and life are directed. Things are ultimately pointed in a certain direction, even though there are many meanderings and deviations from the path, even though there are many rebellions against it. The goal of existence, very difficult of attainment, is the creation of a world freed from oppression, from injustice, from hatred, from strife. History is meaningful because it is the arena where the striving for such a world may take place.

As modern religious believers we accept science, including the theory of evolution. But if evolution were purely accidental, if there were no higher hand influencing it, how strange would it be for a creature to arise who would hear a call for a higher world, who would hear a call to strive for a world of moral perfection. Why not just follow animal instinct? Why the need for higher meaning, for a higher purpose? From science we learn what is. From religion, from the Bible, from revelation, from conscience, the inward revelation, we learn what should be. And it was for this reason, we learn in Genesis, that the Jewish people came into existence, to be a vehicle through which God's higher light and meaning and purpose could shine. It is not that God is concerned with us alone. As He states through the prophet Amos, "O Children of Israel, are you not unto Me like the Ethiopians... have I not taken Israel out of the land of Egypt, the Philistines from Caphtor, and the Arameans from Kir?" The *raison d'etre*, the purpose in the existence of the Jewish people, is to be a means for God's universal vision to be manifest. And this purpose, not realized all at once, requires the allegiance and perseverance of generations. We of this generation are not marooned in time, wondering what we should live for. Rather we are bound to those who have gone before and to those who will come after.

Strikingly, when Jacob in our Parshah, blesses his son, Joseph, he says, "The God in whose presence my fathers walked, Abraham and Isaac, the God who has tended me ever since I was (born), until this day—the messenger who has redeemed me from all ill-fortune, may he bless the lads!" What could this possibly mean? Jacob is speaking to Joseph, one individual, and yet he speaks of "the lads," or a multiplicity of persons. The lads to whom Jacob is referring are Ephraim and Menasheh, Joseph's sons. As Rabbi Isaiah Horowitz, quoted by Plaut, has stated, "There is no greater blessing for a father than the wish that his children should take after him and become good people." Jacob understands that the Jewish project concerns not only his generation, and not only that of Joseph, but all the generations to come, even to the end of time.

This project, which is the ultimate human project, aims to realize, with God's help, those values for the sake of which the world was created. Yet, it comes up against the human capacity for and inclination to evil. No sooner was the first generation of humans procreated, than one son, Cain, murdered another, Abel, out of jealousy. A generation comes into existence which is so steeped in selfishness and disregard for the other, that the best of the lot, Noah, is called good—only for his time. The hurt feeling of a mother, Sarah, leads to a distancing between two brothers, Isaac and Ishmael. Jacob, a son destined for leadership, resorts to trickery to beat out his brother, Esau. And Jacob's sons, envious of their brother, Joseph, first plot his death, and then sell him into slavery to be freed of the threat he posed to their sense of self-esteem.

Still with the tendency to evil there is the impulse and will toward the good. Abraham, the first Jew, pleads with God to save the sinful people of Sodom and Gomorrah. How can you kill the righteous with the wicked, he asks. "Shall not the judge of all the earth act justly?" Esau, the wounded brother, accepts Jacob, reconciling himself to the loss of the "big prize" not only for one election, but for all time. And Joseph, sold into slavery, relinquishes his mask, reveals his true identity, and forgives his brothers, placing love before vengeance, compassion before retaliation.

In this world, laden with God's unrealized purpose, striving for fulfillment, yet confronted by the impulse to evil and egocentricity, we find the good mixed with the bad, the light intermingled with darkness. Customarily, we say that at the point in Jewish history upon which we are focusing the light predominates. When Parshat Vayehi begins, the reconciliation of Joseph and his brothers has already occurred. The people, having escaped famine in Canaan, are not hungry. They have been well received by the Pharaoh. And yet, this picture is overly one-sided and misses the signs that not all is well. Night is already beginning to fall. Joseph, powerful Joseph, wishes to fulfill the request of his father, Jacob, and have him buried in the land of Canaan. Yet, he cannot simply leave. He must ask the Pharaoh and even promise him that he will return. For Pharaoh would not wish to be without his wise viceroy, who is, at one and the same time, his guide and his subject.

Along with his servants and the elders of his household and Egypt, the Pharaoh sends charioteers and horsemen. Clearly, they may serve to protect Joseph and his clan against unfriendly Canaanites. But, in addition, they also serve to guarantee the return of Joseph and his family. Furthermore, the children and the flocks are to remain behind, an added insurance that prized Joseph and the prized Israelites would not abandon the country of their exile. In Hebrew, Egypt is called "Mitzraim," which interestingly has an affinity in sound to another word, "Metzarim," or straits. Egypt has already become a country in which our ancestors have lost their freedom, even if they have not yet been cast into absolute slavery.

Our wish is for liberation. Our wish is for redemption. Our wish is for the attainment of a world of freedom and justice and respect and true humanity. But, at times, both then and now, we see darkness. We may even feel plunged in darkness. But the Bible, whose orientation, as we have seen, is toward the future, discovers sparks of light, even when they may seem absent. The sparks may come from within.

With Jacob dead, Joseph's brothers fear that he will now engage in retribution against them. They do not realize that his reconciliation to them is complete. They go so far as to offer themselves as his slaves. But in speaking with him, they refer to themselves as, "servants of your father's God." In so saying, they demonstrate that they have finally overcome their self-centered concern with status, wondering how they stack up in comparison with their brother. They have finally transcended an absorption with their own feelings and committed themselves to the One who transcends all and is the source of all worthy strivings. In this way, they have engaged in repentance. And thus, from them a light which is inner shines forth.

So, too, a light radiates from the confidence expressed in Joseph's promise—or prophecy—that God will, indeed, take the People of Israel out of the land of Egypt. Perhaps he even intended to symbolically convey this message during the journey to Canaan to bury his father. For the route taken was a circuitous one. The people did not travel by the coast and then head eastward to Hebron for Jacob's burial. Instead, they journeyed toward the east side of the Jordan River, crossing over from there into the land of Canaan. In so doing, as Alter notes, they perhaps mimicked in advance the path of our ancestors following the liberation from Egypt. As long as the spirit does not die, the future is not cut off.

Perhaps fifteen billion years ago a bomb exploded. Perhaps stars and planets and comets and galaxies poured out. And perhaps on this planet, earth, from a slow and gradual process of evolution we emerged. But a higher hand was involved in all this, and through our Torah a recognition of the goal of this cosmic and earthly and human journey has been revealed. That goal, of a perfected world, is not easy of attainment. But even in the presence of darkness, we may be confident that the light, the eternal light, has not been extinguished.

I will close today's sermon with the words of the opening stanza of the Partisans Song, sung by Jewish heroes resisting and fighting the greatest evil which our people and the world has ever seen.

> Say not we have come to the end of the road,
> The day's light has been hidden by the cloud-filled skies,
> Still the day of our longing will grow large and arrive,
> With our footsteps once more shouting, "Here we are.
> We've not died!"

Shabbat Shalom. And may God's peace be our inheritance.

"I HAVE INDEED APPEARED"
A Sermon on Parshat Vaera

Parshat Vaera begins with the following statement, *"Vayedabeir Elohim el Moshe vayomeir eilav, 'Ani YHWH.' Vaera el Avraham el Yitzchak v'el Ya'akov b'El Shaddai ush'mi YHWH lo nodati lahem."* "God spoke unto Moses and said unto him, 'I am YHWH.' I appeared unto Abraham, unto Isaac and unto Jacob as El Shaddai, but by My name, YHWH, I was not known unto them (Ex. 6:2-3)." Now the notion of God appearing is an interesting one. For we do not wish to say that God is ever absent. God is always present, but His presence is not always manifest to us. God is always present, but He does not always emerge out of hiddenness so as to *appear* unto us. In Kabbalah God's Self-hiding, or Self-contraction, as it were, is a condition for there being a world. If God did not curtail the infinite fullness of His presence, there would be no room for anything else to exist. There would not even be room for anyone else to whom God might, at times, appear! And so, God always is, but His presence is not always felt. God always is, but His presence is not always apparent in the immediacy of personal experience.

This notion of something or someone being present without our being aware of it is not really so strange as it might, at first, seem. It is a notion which, in fact, pervades our conception of the world and of ourselves. Think, for example, of the fact that the room where you are this very moment is filled with sound waves of which you have no awareness. Were you to bring in a transistor radio and turn it on, you would become aware of the speech or music waiting to be realized with the aid of a technological device. And even within ourselves we are at all times having unconscious thoughts and feelings of whose existence we are normally unaware. When we make a revealing slip of the tongue, when we have no memory of a painful experience or embarrassing deed, when we have ceased to consciously search for an answer, yet it suddenly flashes before our mind, we become aware of the fact that below the plane of consciousness there stirs a realm of experience and silent meditation. That which truly is does not always appear.

To return to our Parshah, God describes Himself as appearing in different modes. Thus, appearance is not a simple matter, an all-or-nothing thing. God, as it were, has different "profiles" or "faces" through which He may become manifest to us. Neither term is, of course, meant in a literal sense. God is not a bodily being, and even a spiritual "glimpse" of Him is declared impossible. "Man shall not see me and live (Ex. 33:20)." Still God does not always "come across" in the same way. In the passage quoted at the beginning of my remarks He says that He was revealed to the forefathers as "God Almighty," or at least that is the traditional understanding of the name, "*El Shaddai.*" Now He is revealing Himself through the name, "*YHWH,*" meaning that by it He is enabling a new understanding or way of relating to Him which is associated with this name. God as *YHWH* is other than—or more than—God as *El Shaddai*.

Whatever that might mean specifically, a problem immediately thrusts itself before us, and that is what sense we are to make of the statement that God is revealing Himself through a name not known before. For the forefathers did, in fact, use the name, *YHWH*. On the approach of the non-Orthodox Bible critics, the Torah is an editing together of diverse ancient sources. In one source the name, *YHWH*, was known to the forefathers and in another it was not. Our passage from Parshat Vaera comes from the source in which the name, *YHWH*, was first revealed to Moses. The Orthodox approach, which affirms that the Torah comes to us as a unity from Sinai, could not accept such an explanation. Rather what is going on in our passage is that a fuller meaning of the name, *YHWH*, is now being disclosed. Or perhaps that the fuller meaning is being conveyed—or is about to be conveyed — in a more compelling way. God as *YHWH* will be revealed to the entire people through the dramatic events associated with the Exodus from Egypt. Whichever approach is correct, we must still ask, "What is the meaning of this name, of whose correct pronunciation we interestingly do not have certain knowledge?"

For some the name, *YHWH*, formed from the letters, Yod-Hey-Vov-Hey, comes from the root, Hey-Yod-Hey, which means to be. God is *the* Being *par excellence*, the Being not limited in time, the Eternal Being. Such a way of thinking of God is suggested in the hymn, *Adon Olam*, where it is said, "*v'hu haya v'hu hoveh v'hu yihiyeh b'tifara,*" "For He was and He is and He will be in glory." Still in the context in which the name, *YHWH*, is revealed such a meaning seems overly abstract. The people are not attending a seminar in philosophy, where descriptions of the nature of God are being explored. They are sunk in the mud of slavery and await liberation. Not God's being, but His being there would seem to be important. Not God's eternality, but His presence, here and now, would seem to be what matters. And in fact, the great modern Jewish thinker, Martin Buber, says that it is just this which is conveyed by the name, *YHWH*. God is the One who is present. God is the One who does not sit back after bringing the world into existence, simply hoping or "praying" for the best. God is with us in our trials and tribulations. God is a liberating presence, freeing us from slavery and despair.

How does God do this? In the Bible one of the major ways is through the performance of miracles. Events out of the ordinary, events in which a force higher than nature is involved, are a means by which God brings about the goals He intends. The splitting of the Red Sea, or Sea of Reeds, as it has been designated by modern scholars, is an occurrence wrought by God so as to free the People of Israel. It wasn't a lucky coincidence that the sea split at the time that the people, pursued by Pharaoh and his troops, arrived there. It was the result of the divine will that those enslaved go forth to freedom.

It is on this topic, miracles, or more broadly, the direct action of God in the world, that I would like to focus in the remainder of this sermon, while at the end exploring our role in enabling God to appear. I would begin by noting that for many modern people the belief in miracles is not easily achieved. The notion that there are natural causes for events is so deeply ingrained in us that it is difficult to accept the belief that any non-natural force could play a role in bringing about even the most unusual event. Some attempt to escape this difficulty by saying that God planned from the time of creation itself that at a certain moment the Sea of Reeds, for example, would split, allowing a people to become liberated. It was not a coincidence. The naturalistic explanation is not the whole story.

There is an author who "wrote the script" in which it superficially appears that natural forces are the sole cause or effective power. Even the Torah (Ex. 14:21) speaks of "a powerful easterly wind" employed by God to drive the waters of the sea apart. While it occurred suddenly, and only after "Moses stretched his hand over the sea," God still does not simply "barge in" and pull the sea apart. He acts through nature, as it were, enabling an explanatory approach which leaves Him out of the picture. But to do so, to leave God out, is a mistake. We must look beyond appearances. To believe that the People of Israel went forth to freedom just because of a lucky break is too much.

Will such a theological approach work? Does it not seem as if the scientifically sophisticated believer is simply "tacking God onto the explanation" because he feels better if God is there? Are there not times when the Hand of God is needed and no fortunate "coincidence" occurs? Is God absent, or does He not want things to work out in these cases? Perhaps we should simply stick to the scientific explanation and not wonder if there is something more behind the "veil of appearance." Perhaps we should "grow up" and accept the ultimate rule of the impersonal forces of nature.

In exploring the question of miracles further it might be helpful if we look not to an event which is rare, not to the splitting of a sea, but to an event which occurs frequently, one where the scientific explanation is well-known and well-established. I am thinking of an event which has occurred billions of times and where we still, each time it occurs, call it a miracle. It is not that we are in doubt as to its physical causes. It is not that we regard it as "too much" to be a coincidence. It is rather that it is regarded, or better experienced, as something inherently marvelous, intrinsically miraculous. We would regard someone not stirred by the situation as somehow "out of touch," or more precisely, untouched, mysteriously untouched, by what is really there. I am referring to the birth of a child.

Who does not call this a miracle? Yet, who believes that we are in the dark as to its natural causes? Of course, without the process which enables it the phenomenon would not occur. But the phenomenon itself is experienced as stupendous or "mind-blowing." There are those who would argue that the creative hand of God must be seen behind the universe. For there is a very large number of factors which must obtain for life to evolve, and if any one of them was off by even a very slight amount, then life would be impossible. The confluence of all these factors cannot be an accident. Perhaps that is so. But I would suggest that even if fewer factors were needed for life to evolve, and if they could vary by a larger degree, still birth would be miraculous. For a life is not simply a product, a complicated object, which emerges from a prior organism. Through a life we experience more than what goes into its formation at the physical plane. Through a life itself we are in the presence of that which we must term spirit. What do I mean? Consider the following analogy. You take two eggs, crack them and pour them into a frying pan. You add milk and perhaps a little bit of salt and then start stirring. You are preparing scrambled eggs. Suddenly, however, the eggs begin to cry out, "More gently, please. You are stirring too briskly. You know, I have my dignity. You must treat me with respect." What is going on? All we did is mix together some physical substances and here we have a *person*, a being with consciousness and a sense of meaning and of moral right and wrong. Where in the world did all that come in? Is that all simply a byproduct of the physical interactions which give birth to scrambled eggs? To tell the truth, there are those who would apply such an explanation to human beings. Consciousness is nothing more than the "steam," as it were, arising from the behavior of the molecules composing the brain. There is no meaning to existence. The feeling that there is derives simply from the activity of the cells within the brain. Moral sentiments, too, are but the result of biochemical processes in the "gray matter" supposedly distinguishing us as human beings. The brain, physically described, explains all.

But then, what if we do not accept this explanation? What if we find this explanation to be simply unbelievable? It is presented as if it is the rational one. But what if it is not? What if its refusal to go beyond the physical is the result of a *faith-act*, one which refuses to countenance that which cannot be forced into the narrow confines of its naturalistic concepts? If I see a light streaming in through the window, should I conclude that no light is there? Is it just that the window has its own natural radiance? What is "mind-blowing" in birth is that we are in the immediate presence of a person. Perhaps the child does not yet make utterances concerning morality or the meaning of existence. But we find ourselves in the presence of a conscious being, a feeling being, who manifests a unity of personal character and identity even from "day one." Without suggesting that the specific make-up of that personal unity is unrelated to the physical constitution of the person, the very existence of that holistic plane, of that unity of consciousness and temperament, means that more is going on than the interaction of a multitude of separate bodily parts.

A fetus has been formed. But a person has been born. That is the miracle!

I should add that while I do not believe that God intends all of our actions, I do believe that the existence of each individual has been providentially intended. I believe that each individual is unique, and it is that uniqueness, or rather the unique being himself, in his wholeness, who has been intended. Therefore, despite both the similarities between people and the essentially identical process by which people are formed, each birth is a unique event. For it is the beginning of a unique individual, whose particular existence has been intended. Each person is a miracle.

It should be noted in passing that the belief that there is a strict set of laws which does not allow for anything unexpected or surprising has been rejected by modern science. Against those who say that there can never be a return in science to a belief in determinism, or the notion that there is no chance element in the universe, I hold that a restoration of this position is, indeed, possible. But at least in the current view, specifically, within the field known as quantum physics, everything that takes place is not already "inscribed" in the universe as presently constituted. And so, the notion that a miracle is even at variance with the laws of nature is a fiction. Science cannot say what causes one result to occur rather than another, when both lie within the realm of possibility. If the answer is free will, more specifically, divine free will, then what you've got is a—miracle.

Let me continue this digression with a personal story. Some months ago I was thinking about the question of miracles, and after focusing for some minutes on this issue, I pulled out a book called *Quantum Reality: Beyond the New Physics*, by Nick Herbert. I placed it down on our dining room table and, lo and behold, it fell open to the first page of a chapter whose title was, "And Then a Miracle Occurs: The Quantum Measurement Problem." Perhaps this was "just" a coincidence. Or perhaps, as Carl Jung says, there is another principle at work in the universe than the forces of which we typically speak in our scientific investigation. Meaningful conjunctions of events occur. They are not accidental. They are not the product of chance. But venturing further than Jung, I would say that they are the product of Mind. That is, they are evidence of an Intelligence Who is the Source of their occurrence. The mindless "adjudication" between probabilities at the impersonal, physical plane is not all. The active, shaping hand of God is a continuing reality in the universe He has created.

Martin Buber writes,

> The real miracle means that in the astonishing experience of the event the current system of cause and effect becomes, as it were, transparent and permits a glimpse of the sphere in which a sole power, not restricted by any other, is at work.

In other words, the naturalistic explanation continues to provide *its* account of the event. But the event itself is a window through which the presence of a higher light—or better, higher hand—is felt. The event itself is a window to God. If God has created and continues to sustain nature, cannot God through nature awaken us to His living presence? Cannot this itself be part of the miracle, that our awareness cannot be contained within a naturalistic framework, that we ourselves are carried beyond our normal selves?

A miracle does not simply testify to the reality of God. Through a miracle we encounter God, and this, the encounter, is the greatest gift of the miracle. Not simply that we walk across to dry land, not simply that "we live to see another day," but that we are not alone in our journey into the uncertain future. God cries out to Abraham, "Go forth from your land, from your native land, from the home of your father, to the land which I will show you." "What land?," one might ask. "Where am I going? Which road should I take?" Is not every life ultimately a journey upon a "road not taken," with an itinerary which may change any moment? Still we walk not alone. Even through the "valley of the shadow of death... You are with me."

The greatest gift of a miracle is the assurance that a Silent Presence accompanies us in our struggles, in our doubts, in our despair, in our mad affirmation of life, without guarantee, without certitude. The greatest gift of a miracle is the confidence that this "madness," this willing to affirm life over proof, existence over demonstration, has its justification at a plane deeper than mere intellect. We forge ahead, and then we try to figure out. And all the while the Voice within says, "Yes, yes. Say 'yes' to life. Do not stop. For I have not abandoned you, even in the depths of your misery, even when the feeling of hopelessness begins to tempt you." The aftereffects of a miracle may extend even into centuries and millennia beyond, as we know when we consider the saving power of the story of the Exodus.

In closing, let me tell you of Etty Hillesum, a young Dutch Jew, who at the time of the Nazi deportations in Holland volunteered to go to the Westerbork concentration camp. Her goal was to serve her fellow Jews there through work in a hospital. Etty's diaries contain many prayers, and in a striking passage she explains her service to others. *Attempting to console God*, she declares, "we must help You and defend Your dwelling place *in us* to the last."

Deeper than the self is the God Who dwells within. Deeper than the self is the Voice Who is silently heard. Deeper than the self is the Friend Who has never abandoned us.

As we read in the Book of Proverbs, *"ner Hashem nishmat adam,"* "a candle of the Lord is the human soul." There in the innermost soul let us become a 'place' for the dwelling of God. There in the heart's inner recesses let us turn toward the Word which seeks us out. There in the spirit which burns and is never consumed let us hear God proclaim, as He did unto Moses, *"Vaera!,"* "I have, indeed, appeared!"

FROM SLAVERY TO LIGHT
A Sermon on Parshat Bo

In a distant land, far from our shores, there dwelled a people who made their abode, most strangely, in a vast, dimly lit, underground cavern. Rather than turn toward the opening leading out of the cavern, they would sit fixed, gazing toward the innermost wall of their underground abode, watching images produced there by the meager light within. These images they preferred not only to the world awaiting outside the cavern, a world which might be seen in the full light of day, but even to a perception of their neighbors who sat at their very side. Each stared ahead, as if apprehending something of deep and eternal significance. Periodically, the denizens of this submerged world presented their analyses of the images they perceived, competing as to who might demonstrate the greatest brilliance and insight into their ultimate nature and make-up. Fantastic to us, they regarded these images as the real world. Each other they saw as contestants to be outdone and outperformed in the opinions rendered on what were actually mere appearances. They loved these appearances and shied away from really seeing and meeting each other. In darkness they found comfort. In a dungeon from which they might escape they found security.

One day a denizen of this underground cavern, the adopted son of the god-king who ruled the other cave dwellers, struck down his father's chief minister, who had devised a machine to produce ever more fascinating and appealing outer images on which the submerged population gazed. This, his first effort to liberate his compatriots, sunk in slavery and even worshipping slavery, failed, and he, the next in line to rule the cave, fled to freedom, to life in the real world. Years in this world passed, and then a voice began to arise within, instructing him that freedom alone is not sufficient, that without the fellowship of his brothers and sisters in the cave, his life was incomplete, even empty. He returned to the underground cavern, and in a series of striking confrontations with the god-king liberated his people from their abode of darkness. He took them out to a world bathed in light, where they saw the trees and the grass and the hills and the sky. Most importantly, they saw each other.

Our Parshah today, Parshat Bo, is a story of the battle between light and darkness which afflicts the human soul. It is a story of the ever deeper descent into darkness to which people may submit and which they themselves may create. It is a story of the sacrifice of that which is choicest, most precious, in human existence for the illusion of permanent rule over others, others whom one never truly knows, even as one declines further and further in the knowledge of oneself. It is a story of truth versus illusion, of the spirit of God versus evanescent power. It is a story of the service of God versus slavery.

Our story begins with seven plagues having been inflicted upon the people who rule and dominate a kingdom of darkness, a kingdom whose very name, *"Mitzrayim,"* resonates with the overtone, *"Metzarim,"* or narrow places, places of confinement, places in which the human soul and spirit are constricted, even strangled. It is a kingdom built on the subjugation of the stranger by the native-born, a kingdom in which the relation of master and slave, victorious and vanquished in the struggle of life, defines the very character and tone of social interaction. And in our Parshah the consequences of the perception and treatment of the other as but an object to be defeated and dominated descend with ever greater intensity and force upon the ruling population. First, their land is covered with *Arbeh*, or locusts, making it impossible for them to see. Their distorted images of others, of the *B'nai Yisrael*, or Children of Israel, give way to sheer blindness. As the Torah says in describing the locusts, "They hid all the land from view, and the land was darkened."

The word, *"ha'aretz,"* or "the land," we will recall, also means, "the earth" itself, that is, our world. And so, the Torah suggests that in their refusal to let the People of Israel, the subjugated population, go forth to freedom the enslaving rulers finally reached a kind of disconnection from reality, in which they could no longer truly grasp their own situation. This was the inevitable result of an unwillingness to accept their status as human beings created in the image of God rather than as flesh and blood who would be God Himself. In this state, challenged, yet maintaining their power, they retained some ability to function, but were left, at best, flailing about, confused at the threat to their illusion of permanent rule.

Finally, as their spiritual illness reached further, close to the innermost reaches of their very being, they became immobilized, perched on the seat of power, but ready to collapse. For now the true God afflicted them with a *Choshech*, a darkness so deep that they became paralyzed, incapable of action. As the Torah says, "People could not see one another, and no one could get up from where he was..." And yet, with great insight the Torah tells us that those whose lives were not dedicated to domination, to subjugation of their neighbors, could see each other. They were able to see beyond mere images and beyond the blindness, the moral-spiritual blindness which the desire for absolute power begets. They were, miracles of miracles, able to see each other: "but all the Israelites enjoyed light in their dwellings." They who were helpless were able to see their fellows' needs and offer help. From this, from the mutual aid which they gave to each other, they gained the strength for the ultimate liberation, whose goal was the unification of the might needed for self-determination with the *menschlichkeit* needed for the salvation and sanity of the society awaiting creation.

While the Torah speaks of the Almighty's hardening of the heart of Pharaoh, the man who would be God, the same Torah teaches us that, in fact, God has so constructed the human soul that when it sins, when it regards the other as but an opportunity for exploitation, it sets in motion a process which leads to its incapacity to feel and to see the person before one as a fellow creature to whom one is bound. "The eyes are the window of the soul" only to the one who has not only eyes, but a heart with which to see. And if one has not the physical sight with which to see the eyes of the other, one may yet, as we say, be "*Sagi Nahor*," or "rich with light," if one has a soul with which to see.

The darkness in which the *Mitzrim*, the Egyptians, were plunged was not only a physical darkness. The great Jewish mystic, the Maharal of Prague, wrote that the image of God in which the human being is created is perceived in the radiance of the human face. It is not a physical light which shines when one is filled with warmth and concern for the other. It is a spiritual radiance which may be present in the simple smile of a friend or, for that matter, of a stranger whom we encounter on the street. Looking up for a moment our eyes meet and we smile, acknowledging the other whom we have met, acknowledging that for this moment we are together. The outer images we normally see recede like phantasms before a blast of—reality.

Of Moses, the great liberator of the Jewish People, we read, "the skin of his face radiated light," for he made real the image which is no subjective image, the image of God, the spiritual radiance which shines from one hungering for freedom for his fellows trapped in a cave of domination and human forgetfulness. He, the adopted son of the god-king, saw through the eyes of slaves the souls of fellow-children of the true God. He saw the souls of those who were to throw off the chains which were neither their rightful due nor their ultimate destiny. In them he saw not nobodies, but heroic figures poised and ready for the most revolutionary act in human history.

We read, *"Vaya'avidu Mitzrayim et B'nai Yisrael befarech,"* "And the Egyptians oppressed the Children of Israel with crushing hardness." Let us re-read this, "Even within *Metzarim,* even within and in response to confinement, the B'nai Yisrael, the Jewish People, learned *Avodah,* learned how to serve God, not *'befarech,'* not 'in crushing hardness,' but *'befreilach,'* with joy." For suffering though they were, they could see each other and respond. This was their joy. This was their strength, which no human ruler could or can ever destroy. This is the strength which makes of the Jewish People an *"Am Olam,"* an eternal people, connected to the Eternal One Who is deeper than appearances and Who identifies with slaves and liberates them from slavery.

Victims of their own delusive self-exaltation, the Egyptians finally suffer *Makkat Bechorot,* or the slaying of the first-born. But of course! When a generation exists which is dedicated to the domination and destruction of others, which sees only false images and attempts to destroy the people defamed through these images, it either undermines its young or undermines its relation to its young. It either destroys the soul in its young, producing monsters, or destroys its relation to its young who cannot identify with parents who themselves have become monsters. The slaying of the first-born is an act which the *Mitzrim* of every generation wreak upon themselves.

In commemoration of the liberation from Egypt we, in Parshat Bo, receive the Mitzvah of Tefillin. As we read, "And it shall be as a sign upon your hand and as a reminder upon your forehead that with a mighty hand the Lord freed us from Egypt." Why did this act of salvation require such a display of divine might and power? Why could it not be a delicate operation? The answer is that the turning from God and from their human fellows had already become so deep in Pharaoh and his people that only through decisive action could the intolerable condition of slavery and subjugation be ended. As I learned from an extraordinary lay sermonizer, Morris Kleiman, *alav hashalom*, every effort was made to avoid the humiliation of the Egyptian leader. Moses, after all, is commanded, "come to Pharaoh," come to him where he is, speak to him forcefully, but with the respect to which he is accustomed as a human ruler. But Pharaoh's heart was hardened. Indeed, Pharaoh hardened his own heart. Because he lacked the humility which a human being not lost in the darkness of his own egotistical mind would have, he brought about his own crushing humiliation.

The liberation from Egypt, as you know, is so important that God in the first of the *Aseret HaDibrot*, or Ten Commandments, identifies Himself as the God Who took us out of Egypt. A great Hassidic leader, Rabbi Simcha Bunam of Pshischa, was asked, "It is written: 'I am the Lord thy God who brought thee out of the land of Egypt.' Why does it not read: 'I am the Lord thy God Who created heaven and earth'? Rabbi Bunam expounded: 'Heaven and earth!' Then man might have said: 'Heaven—that is too much for me.' So God said to man: 'I am the one who fished you out of the mud. Now you come here and listen to me!'" God is not only the God of cosmic matters and cosmic concerns. God is the God Who is concerned with those who are sunk in the mud of slavery. God is the God Who sees not only slaves, but human beings, Who beholds people not only as winners or losers in a competitive struggle, but as those through whom, through every one of whom, a light, divine in origin, shines.

The great Jewish thinker, Martin Buber, wrote, "Men become what they are, sons of God, by becoming what they are, brothers of their brothers." May we, the House of Israel in this time and place, thank God for the liberation from a submerged world, a cavern-like world of subjugation and blindness, of slavery and delusion. May we turn to each other and, in so doing, confirm that the liberation of time past is a living reality today, inscribed in our mind, in our heart and in all our deeds.

FROM THE SCENE AT SINAI
A Sermon on Parshat Yitro

The most dramatic story in the Parshah of Yitro is that in which the Ten Commandments are given to the People of Israel. There are thunder and lightning and the booming voice of God, which makes the people feel that they are about to die. Smoke billows up from Mt. Sinai, where the people are encamped, and the haze in the horizon is matched by the tremors rippling through their own startled consciousness. God's great statement for human existence is about to be delivered, beginning with His demand of loyalty from these slaves whom He has only recently liberated. We feel that the description of the preparations and context for these words to be revealed is fitting, given their weight and significance in national and human affairs. And our focus upon them is both enabled and intensified by the vivid characterization of the natural and human setting in which they are to be disclosed.

Contrary to normal expectation, I do not wish to focus upon the contents of the ten great utterances which were heard at Sinai. Rather I shall concentrate on the aforementioned scene itself as a source of teaching and illumination concerning human existence. Admittedly, I shall encounter the description, in part, through the prism of meaning which has developed in the later elaboration of Jewish life and tradition. Yet, even there, I believe, the lesson to be unfolded is already latent in the text. The words used, in both their original and later meanings, contain hints about life at its most authentic, about existence in its most fully realized spiritual form. They do not simply paint a scene. They send a message. And the message entails fundamental insights about the human soul and its redemption from both spiritual aloneness and social disharmony. It is not simply that the "medium is the message." More than a feeling or sensibility is being conveyed and generated. The medium is a fount from which the spiritual message itself may come forth. The medium is the ground from which a new way may be recognized and realized.

Let us begin with the description of the scene at Sinai, found in Exodus 19:16-19.

And behold, on the third day, at morning time, there were thunder and lightning and a dense cloud over the mountain, and a very powerful blast of the horn, and all the people who were in the camp trembled. Moses took the people out from the camp toward God, and they stood at the foot of the mountain. Now Mount Sinai was filled with smoke, for the Lord had descended upon it in a fire, and the smoke rose up like the smoke of a kiln, and the entire mountain trembled greatly louder, ever louder, grew the blast of the horn; Moses spoke, and God answered him in a thunderous voice.

It is fascinating to note that the term for horn in the above passage is *shofar*. It may, of course, be understood in a purely naturalistic way, as referring to a powerful wind, whose howling sounds like the blast of a horn. But at the same time, the use of this term to describe a wind is suggestive to us. For a *shofar*, in its most frequent usage, is a ram's horn, such as we blow on the High Holidays, reminding us to engage in the act of *teshuvah*, or repentance. In one sense, this means the repentance for the commission of sins. Each deed is important, and for our wrongful deeds we need both to experience and express regret and to commit ourselves to a changed pattern of behavior in the future.

Teshuvah in its literal meaning, however, signifies return. It, thus, suggests our coming back to something or someone with whom we're already familiar. It refers to the restoration of a bond or relationship which has already existed, but which we have weakened or broken. It presupposes that we have become estranged, perhaps so deeply that we have even ceased to be aware of our estranged state. We are now trying not only to make amends, but to mend the relationship with the one we have turned from and forgotten, so as to hopefully bring the relationship to an even higher level than that it was at prior to the estrangement.

Let me give you a contemporary—but not only contemporary— example. A person, despite success in his profession, despite the love of family and the friendship of many, despite the good health of all those dear to him and the respect of the community, begins to feel a spiritual hunger. Something, he senses, is missing in his life, and he begins to embark upon a search for a source of ultimate fulfillment, a source of ultimate meaning and purpose. Success, well-being, pleasure, social accolades are not enough. "What is the point of this venture called 'life?,' he asks. "One day I showed up in this world. Someday, hopefully not in the near future, I will take leave of it, or simply cease to be. Does my being here make any ultimate difference? Is it important that I live in a particular way, not because it will make me feel better, but because my actions, my deeds, are needed for the realization of some higher meaning, some not-humanly-created meaning? These questions assail the person for whom success and well-being are, by themselves, not enough. The possibility of despair before their inadequacy is a condition for the venture beyond to where the command from on high becomes a call felt within. This is the venture of homecoming, of return, to which we are awoken by the blast of the *shofar*, not a mere desert wind, but a voice which, with urgency, says, "Come back. I await you. The path of redemption is here and seeks out your authentic liberation."

From a religious point of view the yearning for meaning, the hunger, the quest, is a sign of an already existing relation to God, the source of ultimate meaning. We experience a pull back at the conscious level to the One in whom originates a fulfillment going beyond any which might be achieved through work or social relationship alone. It is not that the search for and service to a higher purpose need carry us away from an engagement in these spheres of life, but it includes them within a wider, even infinite, framework. It infuses them with a transcendent meaning which they lack when they are viewed as only human endeavors. God, on this view, is the Magnet who draws us back to Him and, in so doing, draws us to our higher selves.

Etymologically, the term, "religion," means to bind back. Thus, *teshuvah*, in its largest sense, is of the very essence of religion. The *shofar* sound which was heard at Sinai is meant to stir up in us and strengthen an awareness of our inner tie to God. The *shofar* which was heard at Sinai is telling us, "Turn back to your origin, to the Place which is your spiritual home. Turn back to the Place from which you can never truly depart, though in your sleep you may become oblivious to its presence. Turn back by venturing out beyond yourself in the direction of an encompassing Other who is both the soil of

Davin Wolok

self-transcendence and the ground of true self-realization. Turn back and touch that which is eternal, becoming liberated from the terror of time, the ephemerality and transience of finite existence. Turn back and discover—life."

Still how may this turning be achieved? The answer to this question must take into account the fear which stands in the way of turning, or more precisely, which makes it difficult. This difficulty is hinted at in Exodus 19:17, where we read, "And Moses took the people out of the camp toward God, and they stood at the foot of the mountain." We might have expected to find the verb, "*vayavei*," "and he brought," rather than the verb, "*vayotzei*," "and he took out," used to describe Moses' behavior. Is he not simply moving his people to a spot close to the mountain, where they will hear the word of God? No. Moses is engaged in something much more significant than that. The root of the verb, "*vayotzei*," "*yod-tzadi-alef*," is identical to that of "*hotzeiticha*," the word used in the Ten Commandments when God describes Himself as the One who *took us out* of slavery. The people are being moved from one state of being to another—or at least an attempt in this direction is being made. The people are still stuck in the more contracted and reduced sense of self which a slave develops. "I am a nobody. I am a mere object to be used by others for their purposes. I am only a means to an end, not a true agent, whose actions may be in the service of the highest values, rather than the mere whims of another human being." Moses is trying to take the people out from their self-denigrating slave mentality, to enable the encounter with God which is both a cause and a result of an authentic, liberated sense of self. There is security in knowing who I am, even if that I is so suppressed that one cannot say it fully is.

To relinquish a constricted sense of self generates anxiety and even terror. One may feel one is abandoned unto—or even becoming—nothingness. "Where am I? Who am I? Can I survive?" Indeed, if a human has within a spark of the infinite, he is yet a finite being, and a too direct, too uncontained, encounter with the ultimate source of his being, with the infinite God himself, may be beyond his finite capacities. "Man shall not see Me and live," says God. Still the alternative is not to stay mired in a mode of being which falls far short of our full humanness. Moses must extract the people from their reduced, self-denigrating state. He must take them out of that state toward a level of being of which they are capable and in which they shall become truly themselves. He is a shepherd taking his flock to a new spiritual plane. He is a physician of the soul seeking to heal the depressed spirits of those he tends. He is a midwife, enabling the birth of his people, their exodus from the womb of a reduced status and reduced self-image. He does not simply bring the people. He pulls them out. He takes them forth. He leads them to an encounter with the Source of their existence, the Fount of their spiritual redemption, their Liberator and Friend, God.

Teaching, virtually compelling courage, Moses leads the people to an encounter in which the means of returning them to their true spiritual identity is not an education of the mind alone. In fact, apart from the contents of the revelation they shall receive, there is the reality of the experience of revelation itself, that is, of the self-presentation of God to them. A living encounter takes place. They are confronted by God, who in His first declaration identifies Himself as their liberator, as the One who rescued them from misery and oppression. There is not the imparting of information alone. There is a meeting, a charged meeting, of the Divine Person and the people upon whom He shall thrust a special task and destiny.

In order to be changed in life we must be touched at a level deeper than reason. We may be told that we are of value. But acts of kindness and deeds imbued with respect send the message more powerfully and indelibly. Sometimes the means of affecting us reaches beneath the level of language. Music may stir us and arouse the unquenchable sense that life has meaning, even though nothing tangible has been uttered or enunciated. But even when words are employed, the presence, the direct presence, of the other to us matters as much as, and often more than, the concepts conveyed through the medium of speech.

God does not simply make Himself present in order to engage in the act of revelation. God's making Himself present is itself an act of revelation. Mind alone is not addressed. The self, the soul, of the people is shaken out of its spiritual slumber by the confrontation with God, the One who breaks through their defenses and intrudes Himself into their innermost being. It is not that they will not try to flee from this encounter. It is not that they will cease forever to try to turn away. But they have now been pulled into a relationship, and turning from a relationship is not the same as rejecting a piece of advice or instruction. In trying to return the people to their true spiritual selves God does not rule out the possibility of backsliding. But He employs a directness and a forcefulness which is absent in an appeal to the intellect alone. God wants to break through the barriers of the self. He wishes to galvanize the soul and offer the felt, lived opportunity to turn back, finding both peace and God together.

It should not be thought that the experience of a dramatic impact by something or someone greater than us is a phenomenon to be found in the realm of religion alone. In describing his own act of creation, Beethoven, for example, said the following.

> What we conquer for ourselves through art is from God, divine inspiration.... Every genuine creation of art is independent, mightier than the artist himself, and through its manifestation, returns to the Divine. With man it has only this in common: that it bears testimony to the mediation of the Divine in him.

Surprisingly, even Nietzsche, not a believer in God, described his experience of inspiration in the following way:

> one becomes nothing but a medium for supermighty influences. That which happens can only be termed revelation; that is to say, that suddenly, with unutterable certainty and delicacy, something becomes visible and audible and shakes and rends one to the depth of one's being. One hears, one does not seek, one takes, one does not ask who it is that gives; like lightning a thought flashes out, of necessity, complete in form.... It is a rapture... a state of being entirely outside oneself.... Everything happens in the highest degree involuntarily, as in a storm of feeling, freedom, of power, of divinity.

That the encounter of which Nietzsche speaks is one of revelation was emphasized by the Jewish religious philosopher, Martin Buber, in his seminal work, *I and Thou*, when he wrote,

> we receive what we did not have before us in such a manner that we know: it has been given to us. In the language of the Bible: "Those who wait for God will receive strength in exchange." In the language of Nietzsche who is still faithful

to actuality in his report: "One accepts, one does not ask who it is who gives.

In our scientific culture there is a prejudice toward what we can learn in an ordinary, uninspired state of consciousness. And this we want to be able to confirm through repetitions of experience at this plane, for example, through experimentation. But are there not singular experiences which break through the habitual scheme in which things appear? Are there not unique states of being which call into question the adequacy of our usual framework of explanation? When two people, for example, feel a direct soul-to-soul contact, notwithstanding spatial separation, is it possible that visual perception does not tell the whole story? Is it possible that a level of awareness is opened up which escapes the grasp of vision by the eyes alone? And perhaps that level, of depth and spiritual richness, of truth which refuses to be encompassed by masks and appearances, is there all the time, not as consciously realized, but as a balm and fulfillment waiting to be awoken.

The hope that we can get in touch with this plane of true meeting is suggested by the use of a particular term when the revelation at Sinai ceases. For in Exodus 19:14 we read of the people, "When the ram's horn sounds a long blast, they may go up on the mountain." During the revelation itself they are forbidden to so ascend. Yet, the mountain is not inherently holy. Its holiness derives only from God's presence on it during the revelation, and with this concluded, going up is permitted. The term for ram's horn in this instance is *yovel*, which also means jubilee, or the final year in a fifty-year cycle, at which time land which was originally owned by a family is returned to it. None should on a permanent basis own more than another. Ultimately, there must be a sense of equality and fellowship, a sense which should continue even when outward inequalities creep in, even when estrangement and opposition block a feeling of partnership and connectedness. Before God we are all equal, a fellowship, each of whose members is created in His image. Before God we are not separate islands. Nor should we be so to each other.

Can a sense of fellowship be tasted more often? Can we appreciate each other and God's world more regularly? Judaism, I would suggest, is a religion of hope and possibility. We are not fated to remain stuck in patterns of behaving and relating which are unfulfilling. There is choice. The challenge is to pull ourselves out of an unfruitful mode of being brings to mind the great American classic, *Our Town*, by Thornton Wilder. In it a woman, Emily, who has died young, is allowed to return to this world to relive one day of her life. After witnessing with greater awareness the life we live, she cries out,

I can't. I can't go on. Oh! Oh. It goes so fast. We don't have time to look at one another.

She asks a character called the Stage Manager,

Do any human beings ever realize life while they live it? — every minute?

The Stage Manager says,

No.

The saints and poets, maybe—they do some.

May we, the Children of Sinai, hear the blast of the Shofar, summoning the courage to return to that realm where lie peace and true fulfillment, with gratitude for the world God has given, with appreciation for the time we have—each other.

FAITH IN THE JOURNEY
A Sermon on Parshat Masei

A man enters a travel agency and says to the agent who greets him, "I would like to go on a vacation." "Well, where would you like to go?," responds the agent. "I'm not sure. What do you recommend?" "How about France?," says the agent. "Oh no," says the man. "I'm Jewish, and in 1182 my people were expelled from France." "Well then, how about England?," says the agent. "Oh no," says the man. "In 1290 we were expelled from England." "Well then, how about Spain?" "Oh no," says the man. "In 1492 we were expelled from Spain."

Suddenly, the phone rings, and the agent brings the man a globe and says to him, "Listen, you look at the globe and when I'm done with the call, you'll tell me where you want to go." The agent takes the call, then comes back to the man and asks, "So, where would you like to go?" The man responds, "Do you have another planet?"

Our Parshah today, Parshat Masei, begins by recounting all of the travels of our ancestors, the Children of Israel, in the Wilderness of Sinai. Every place they departed from and every place they came to is mentioned. While they did not travel at a fast clip, their life was at the same time, not a static one. Movement, change, bumps in the road, crises, challenges, moments of peace followed by moments of danger, were their lot. But in this whole adventure, they knew where they were headed, or rather, as they found out, where, at least, their children would arrive, the land of Canaan, the Promised Land, destined to become the Land of Israel.

We might imagine that when they finally arrive, there will be a less unsettled existence. But what do we discover? Laws concerning what to do if someone accidentally kills another and a relative of the deceased wishes to wreak vengeance upon the manslayer. Cities of refuge are to be erected to which the manslayer may flee and remain unharmed by the raging relative. Interestingly, when the *Kohen Gadol*, or high priest, dies the manslayer may leave the city and remain unharmed. The implication is that in the face of the societal tragedy, the emotions of the relative toward the manslayer will become cooled and his desire for vengeance will dissipate.

What I wish to emphasize, however, are not the specifics of the case under question, but the fact that even arriving in the Promised Land and settling there does not mean you have a settled existence. Tragedy may yet occur. Emotions may fly out of control. There is no guarantee that you will not need protection against those who allow themselves to be possessed by irrational anger and hatred. The need to cope, to move on, to meet new challenges, in other words, the way of life when you were striving for the home, or world, of your dreams, does not cease when you have arrived there. One day, we hope, a world of perfection will be realized. But until then there is always a mix of the good and the bad, the fulfilling and the tragic, the uplifting and the saddening. Even after we "settle in," life remains a journey.

This fact, that in a world in which we find a measure of that which we legitimately seek, we also encounter evil and absurdity, poses a challenge to any human being who wishes to make sense of his or her own existence. Why is this world here? Why am I here? Is there any meaning behind the perplexing situation in which I find myself? Do I, does the world, fulfill any purpose by existing?

The Jewish pattern of ritual and communal life provides a framework in which people may experience increased inner peace and human interconnectedness, both aids in coping with the challenges and difficulties of life. I shall conclude today's sermon with a concrete case in which the benefit of this way of life may be tasted. But before then I wish to focus on what is, in fact, the foundation of this way of life, namely, the faith-commitment without which Judaism is simply, in large measure, a collection of customs, an etiquette for social and individual existence. As such, it would not be without value. Reciting *Hamotzi* at the beginning of a meal would still help to create a feeling of fellowship between people eating together. Lighting candles on Friday evening would still remind us to take a break from the mad rush of our "normal" weekday lives.

But obviously there is more to Judaism than this, and obviously Judaism came from and is founded on more than this, however truly important it is. In discussing Judaism the question of faith must be addressed and in confronting it, I believe, we will receive a strength which we can gain from nowhere else. In this sermon I will focus only on one element of Jewish faith, namely, the individual's faith in God. Such faith, we know, involves a recognition of our responsibilities to others as fellow children of God. Judaism, after all, is the source of a vision of a world of ultimate social harmony and justice. But the faith-affirmation itself, which began with one individual, Abraham, is what I want to concentrate on here.

So, what am I to believe? There is much that would turn us in the direction of a faith is God. Interestingly, in our scientific age it may, in certain ways, be easier to believe in God than in the past. Science, for example, argues that the world came into existence out of an original explosion, a "big bang," before which nothing existed. There was no matter. There was nothing which came together and exploded. Rather there was a radical beginning. The world began, but from where? And how? As Arno Penzias, an astronomer who demonstrated the truth of the big bang theory, explained, this theory obviously points us in the direction of a divine creator of the universe, or God. I might note that Penzias is a Conservative Jew, though clearly what he said makes sense regardless of one's particular religious orientation.

Then there is the fact that the universe seems to be fine-tuned for life. If even one of the physical factors which make life possible were off to the most infinitesimal degree, life would never have come about. Atheists, facing this fact, say that there may be an infinite number of universes, each with a different character, and we're just in the lucky one. But what evidence is there for these infinite other universes? The fine-tuning of the universe for life suggests that Someone, namely, God, did the fine-tuning. This does not mean, however, that evolution did not occur. To the contrary, evolution was the means through which the miracle of life became realized.

Then there are the uplifting experiences we have of nature, which suggest to us that the world has a higher source. Many people in the presence of the Grand Canyon, for example, speak of their awe before this exalting scene and their sense that there must be some author, or artist, who brought about this amazing display, working through natural law. Finally, there is our own inner moral sense, the voice of conscience within, telling us that certain things are absolutely right or wrong and not simply a matter of human feeling or opinion. Where did this higher sense come from? Once again we are pointed in the direction of God.

But then, as I have noted, there are also experiences of evil and absurdity. The Holocaust is the most extreme example which we would mention in this regard, but as the author, Dostoevsky, noted, even the death of one child is a challenge to God. How could a good God, a God who not only authors nature, but instills us with conscience, allow such a tragedy?

So, what are we to do? If there is no God, then the world makes no sense. Its existence makes no sense. Its order makes no sense. Its beauty and glory make no sense. The presence of conscience within us makes no sense. Is there any other piece of evidence which will help us? For faith is not legitimate if it cannot make sense to or be accepted by one who has experienced the worst.

In raising this issue, I recall an experience I had with my cousin, Celia Levinsky, a survivor of the Holocaust. Celia and I were standing in front of her house, I believe it was after returning from shul one Shabbat, and in explaining her faith, she said to me, "What am I, a monkey?" Now today we may say that animals have greater worth than was normally believed in the past. But Celia's meaning was clear. She was saying that she had an inner, inextinguishable, gut feeling that she was more than a mere biological creature, that while she was flesh and blood, she was more than flesh and blood. She was a being who had a meaning, a purpose, a worth, and therefore there must be a source for that meaning and purpose and worth, or God.

Now one may say that this was a mere feeling, and a feeling doesn't prove anything. And yet, with only the fewest exceptions, generally of people suffering from a clinical depression, people have this feeling. Even people who say there is no God have this feeling. They may deny God, but their feeling about themselves, like Celia's about herself, makes sense only if there is a higher source of meaning, or God. Furthermore, this feeling, and the faith that comes from it, may be maintained even in the face of evil and untold suffering. But how? The Bible, not shrinking from a confrontation with this problem, speaks to us of the case of Job, a good man who undergoes horrendous suffering, but who is lifted up beyond his suffering when God reassures him that there is meaning, even if he—and we—cannot grasp it in our human terms or concepts. We do not have to understand why suffering is part of life in order to affirm that life, all of it, is meaningful, that God is, indeed, present.

Interestingly, such a faith may have the most practical of results, though I am not suggesting we should believe only because of its results for us, which would then make it have ultimately a self-focus and not a God-focus. Nonetheless the practical benefits of faith are real and have explored and elucidated by a distinguished medical researcher in our own area, Dr. Herbert Benson. What Benson discovered was that even on the physical level faith helps to promote well-being. It is not a guarantee. It is not a foolproof protection against illness. If it were, there would be no fatal conditions. But all things being equal, faith helps, both in healing and in coping with illness when healing does not occur. For those who survive faith is an antidote and a support, even at the physical plane.

As Benson writes, "I am astonished that my scientific studies have so conclusively shown that our bodies are wired to believe, that our bodies are nourished and healed by prayer and other exercises of belief. To me, this capability does not seem to be a fluke; our design does not seem haphazard... . My reasoning and personal experience lead me to believe there is a God." It could, of course, be a coincidence that faith seems to sustain us. But normally speaking, capacities are beneficial only if they put us more fully in touch with reality. A hand which can touch is of benefit only because there are things to pick up. Eyes are of benefit only because there are things to see. Perhaps, in like measure, there is a spiritual environment, a divine presence, to which we relate through faith, and in doing so, we do better.

This discovery, I should add, has been a major factor in the success of Alcoholics Anonymous, which calls upon the recovering alcoholic to recognize the presence in his or her life of a Higher Power, a God from whom he or she receives support and guidance. In the words of the Psalmist, "Cast your burden upon God, and He will sustain you." The sustenance, it must be admitted, will not always be what we regard as a practical solution to our problem. What we dearly and legitimately wish for will not always occur. But feeling strengthened in the face of our problem, in the face even of tragedy, is also sustenance dearly needed. And when we feel that that sustenance and the strength it provides is lacking, we should nonetheless persevere. I am struck by the fact that even one of the great Hassidic masters,

Rabbi Nachman of Bratslav, at times felt the absence of God. Faith, palpably felt, may not be a constant. There may be a wrestling and a recommitment. But in that way, the faith-relationship to God is like many relationships, in which there is an ebb and a flow, intimacy, at times estrangement and then reconnection.

I earlier said that in this sermon I was not going to focus on the role of ritual in our spiritual life. And yet, to totally leave it out would perhaps be strange for your ritual director. And so, I am going to conclude by noting the role which the Minyan and the recitation of Kaddish may have in our faith-life. I will do so by quoting from a book entitled, *The Kaddish Minyan: The Impact on Ten Lives*. It was edited by Rabbi Herbert Yoskowitz, one of the rabbis of my family's shul in Detroit. In the book ten congregants comment on their own experience of reciting Kaddish, and I shall quote from the selection written by Bill Graham. Bill writes,

"Ten months ago, our seventeen-year-old daughter, Alex, died of cancer.... After our daughter died, coming to morning services and saying Kaddish was the most natural thing for me to do. It was a way to honor her memory and, more importantly, it was a way for me to reaffirm my faith in God.... I am at peace during Kaddish; I feel as if I am a *tallit* and I am wrapping myself around her, giving her comfort. In reality, I know that she is the one that is giving me comfort.... I say Kaddish as a means of honoring our daughter and gaining comfort, but, most of all, reaffirming my faith in God. It is my faith that has given me the strength these past two years. If it were not for my faith in God, I would never have been able to handle this tragedy."

In our journey through life, in our travels from one unexpected moment to another, let us make ourselves available to the strength which comes from an openness to the spiritual environment within which we dwell, the divine field who is both our source and our sustenance. "May God give strength unto His people; may God bless His people with peace."

A PARSHAH OF WORDS
A Sermon on Parshat Devarim

It was July 3, around 10:30 A.M., and my wife, Carol, and I were sitting in the Paris Café at Coolidge Corner. Carol was having a cranberry-flavored Cape Codder Smoothie and I was having a cup of coffee, half decaf, half regular. Suddenly, ideas for this Dvar Torah burst into my mind. I rapidly wrote them down on the paper I had, as well as on three napkins I borrowed from the Paris. The talk you are about to hear had its beginning in that café-inspired moment of illumination.

Our Parshah today, Parshat Devarim, begins with the statement, "*Eileh hadevarim asher diber Moshe el kol Yisrael b'eiver haYarden*," "These are the words which Moses spoke to all Israel across the Jordan," that is, on the east side of Jordan River, where our ancestors waited before they advanced into the Promised Land. It should not be supposed, however, that the words being referred to are only those which begin or even compose the bulk of Parshat Devarim, whose literal meaning—by the way — is "A Parshah of Words." Rather the reference is to almost the entirety of the book to come, that is, Sefer Devarim, or the Book of Words. For this, the fifth book of the Torah, is comprised, in essence, of Moses' farewell addresses to the people, with God's instruction for the life they are to lead in the land of their and His dreams.

Given the unique character of our book, I would like to focus in today's Dvar Torah upon the power—or powers — of words in human life. An examination of the range of meanings of the term, "*Devarim*", in Biblical Hebrew itself suggests the presence of a powerful force in human existence. For "Devarim" means not only words, but also events, happenings. It signifies something alive, dynamic, involving change. It is not static. It is not, God forbid, dead. It has an impact, creative and momentous. Let us recall that it is by words that God, according to Genesis, brings the world into existence. As we have recounted in our prayers, "*Baruch she'amar v'hayah haolam*," "Praised be He who spoke and the world erupted into being." It is in recognition of the dignity of a human being that he is called by medieval Jewish philosophers, "*hamedaber,*" "the one who speaks." In speaking we have a likeness to God. We are not simply a created object, a stone or pebble, buffeted about by wind and storm. We can comment on things and conceive in words imaginative responses to our situation in the world.

Some people think that the only thing that counts is physical force. So, they may say, "Sticks and stones can break my bones, but words can never hurt me." But how shallow and shortsighted is such an approach. For words can have a greater impact than physical objects. As is noted in Pirkei Avot, the Ethics of the Fathers, a humiliating word can destroy another human being. It can make it impossible for that person to hold his head high or even show his face in public. True, sufficient physical force can, God forbid, bring about the end of a person's life. But even in facing his demise, if this person says, as we did while taking the Torah out of the ark, "*ana avda deKudsha Brich Hu,*" "I am a servant of the Holy One Blessed Be He," then he will die with self-esteem. Conversely, a person who says, "I am a nobody," may feel dead even while alive. A word can lift a troubled spirit. A word can comfort a distressed mind. And so, I say, it is with supreme wisdom that the Torah places a special emphasis upon words. The discourse to follow is, in essence, a meditation upon words.

I have noted how, according to the Torah, God created the world through words. But beyond this, words may be the means by which a relationship comes into being. They may be the means by which not only a promise is made, but through which partners promise themselves to each other. In a Yom Kippur piyyut, or poem-prayer, we read, "*anu ma-amirecha v'Atah ma-amireinu,*" which means, "we pledge ourselves to You (O God), and You pledge Yourself to us." Interestingly, the word to pledge, "*ma-amir,*" comes from the Hebrew root, "*Alef-Mem-Reish,*" which means, "to say." So, in reality, the prayer affirms our saying that we are God's, and God's saying that He is ours. It sounds something like a wedding ceremony, does it not?

Words are, of course, the vehicle of every promise. And note the power of a promise in the human heart. I do not mean that promises are never broken. But one who has made a promise in truth is unable to break it even if the one to whom he made it has passed from this earth. A man promises his father that he shall fulfill a particular obligation. Before he has time to complete the fulfilling of this obligation his father, hopefully after a long and healthy life, dies. There is not in this world anyone to whom to keep the promise. He is gone, and yet the man feels that he owes it to his father to keep it. In fact, perhaps the father only asked the son on his deathbed to fulfill some task. There was no chance that it could be fulfilled before the final goodbye. Still to not fulfill the task, to not keep the promise, would be felt to be spiritual suicide by one not already spiritually dead. I should note that according to John Findlay, the late Boston University philosopher, this sense that a promise must be kept, even beyond death, itself suggests that deep within we have an intimation that death is not the final end. Whether or not he is right, I think it is clear that we do not regard one who is dead as simply "dead and gone." In a promise one heart is linked to another forever.

Now in speaking of promises I have not mentioned something which is so obvious that it would not seem to need mentioning. And that is the particular kind of words which come into play between the participants in a promise. I am not, however, referring to the words which describe the content of the promise. I am not referring to what it is you say you will do. I am simply pointing to the fact that each person in the relationship is called by a name. Names, names, my God, this is the very name of an entire book of the Torah, the second book, in Hebrew, *Shemot*. Let me suggest that if we had a full description of a person, but no name for her, then we would feel something is terribly missing. Yet, if we had only a name, but no description, it would still feel like it is a person of whom we are speaking.

This happened to me once. I attended a wedding in the old Vilna Shul, and as I was walking out I saw over the entrance a plaque with the names of deceased members of the shul. I had no idea who these people were. But it felt so good that their names were inscribed. They lived. They were here. They were not nobodies. They were beings who had names. A name can express and crystallize a whole personality. "That's Debby," we say. "That's Sam. That's Martha." A name can even help make a fictional character seem like someone who lived. "What was Hamlet really like?," we ask. "What made him tick? Why was he so conflicted?" Once while teaching a class in graduate school I began to say regarding another figure, "Huckleberry Finn was one of the most beautiful men in American history." In mid-sentence I stopped. I all of a sudden remembered that he had never lived.

Fiction, I should note, is but one example—though a very important example—of how through words we lift ourselves above our immediate experience and envision things anew. It is clear that for me—and not only me—Huckleberry Finn means hope and friendship and freedom and equality. But you and I can ourselves use words so as to liberate ourselves from what we feel is unavoidable pain. I do not mean that through words we can magically dispel all anguish. I do not mean that words are a wand which we wave over any terrible situation and make it good. But words can ease pain and hold open the door for better possibilities. We may, for example, describe one and the same situation as "overwhelming" or "challenging," even "extremely challenging." We may portray one and the same circumstance as "devastating" or "trying," even "extremely trying." Believe me. I do not wish to make light of the horrors which human beings at times face in our world. But words, words, can lighten the burden at least a bit, and budge open the door where a new future may await us.

Sometimes simply by expressing our pain in words, sometimes simply by verbalizing what we feel, we help to lighten our burden. Scientists do not yet know why this is so. But clearly it is. Even a complete form of psychotherapy may center on putting into words one's bottled up emotions. Somehow we begin to gain power over what seemed impossible to deal with when we can describe it freely, frankly, without embarrassment or shame. Words are a force for liberation.

In saying this, however, I do not want to suggest that words are the be-all and end-all. Sometimes the pain is so great that we accept the need for silence. Thus, when visiting a house of Shiva our tradition counsels us to not address the mourner first, but let him commence conversation, if he so wishes. Perhaps he still needs to abide with his feelings and utterance in words is not possible. At the same time, in such a situation all words by the one attempting to bring comfort fall short. I do not suggest that they should not be said. But it should not be imagined that they will be as adequate as in everyday situations. Sometimes the most comforting thing to say to a mourner is simply, "I know there are no words."

At the same time, in human life words may fall short not only because of immense pain. Words may also fall short because of sublime wonder, because of majesty and exaltation. In Psalm 19 we read both, "The heavens declare the glory of the Lord," and "there is no utterance, there are no words, no sound is heard." In pain we cannot speak. In radical amazement we are speechless. Face to face with a friend, too, we may find that even as the result of a good conversation words die away. We feel no need to fill the ensuing silence with chatter. We are so comfortable with each other. We are so at one each with the other. There is no need to speak. The silence almost feels like a haven of peace. The silence almost feels like the fulfillment of speech. Not its opposite, but its complement, its kissing cousin.

Is there any further element upon which we must focus in our meditation today upon the multifaceted world of words? Yes, and this includes both utterance and quiet. I am referring to the fact that speech involves sound. Wait a minute, you may say. How, if I speak of sound, can I mention quiet? The reason is, of course, that sound is not continuous. When we speak, there are pauses. And pauses in the right places add to the effect of the speech. As for the speech, it entails a range of sounds. Rare, indeed, is the speech which is truly in a monotone. Were it to occur, how painful it would be to listen to? Are not "monotone" and "monotonous" related? So, good speech involves the effective use of sound. It must be pleasing to the ear and even riveting to the heart. But how, if that is the case, can Moses have been an effective speaker? We learn in the Book of Shemot, the Book of Names, that Moses was a stutterer. Can he have been the grand orator of the Book of Devarim, the Book of Words?

Some may suppose that by the time our ancestors reached the threshold of the Promised Land Moses had overcome his speech impediment. It is said of Demosthenes, the ancient Greek orator, that he had had to overcome such a difficulty. His method of doing so was of standing by the seashore with pebbles in his mouth and trying to speak. I wonder how many modern-day speech pathologists would employ this technique. At any rate, I do not see why we must suppose that Moses had to cease being a stutterer in order to deliver the wonderful speeches of Devarim. Some years ago I heard Professor Benjamin Schwartz, of blessed memory, the renowned Harvard Asian studies scholar, speak. At times, between sentences, while looking for a word, he would go, "uh, uh, uh, uh." As my friend, Dr. Maurice Tuchman, who was with me noted, these "uhs" drew you in. What was Ben going to say now? What was this phenomenally brilliant man going to state? Sound is important. The soul of Moses was heard within his stammer and without.

Now you know that we consider sound very important when we read the Torah. For we do not simply read. We sing, as Dan Desatnick did so beautifully today. And the musical symbols which are used to guide one performing this task are called "trop." Each one stands for a pattern of sounds which is to be fused with the word pronounced. Another name for the trop, however, is "*ta-amei haMikrah*," which literally means, "the tastes of Scripture." Why do they have this name? I would suggest it is because the Torah is meant to touch us in a felt, almost physically felt way. We are to taste it, to take it in, to digest it, to make it part of ourselves. For this it needs to have a flavor.

And with that thought in mind, I would now like to close this Dvar Torah, this meditation upon the sacred domain of words, by asking my wife a question. "Carol, can I have a sip of your smoothie?"

Thank you—and Shabbat Shalom.

FOR LIFE AND ETERNITY ARE JOINED EACH INTO THE OTHER
A Sermon in Response to Parshat Ki Tetzei

Our Parshah today begins with the words, "*Ki tetzei lamilchamah ahl oivecha*," "For if you should go out to war against your enemies." In so doing, it immediately turns our attention to a tragic phenomenon within human life, namely, the battle of human brother against brother. Not being pacifistic in orientation, the Torah does not say that one should never go out to war. In fact, one may even be obligated to go out to war. Israel's recent war against Hezbollah, I believe, falls within that category. Yet, the necessity to wage war against one's fellow human beings does not eliminate the fact that the entire phenomenon of war, of the battle of human brother against brother, is tragic.

As Adam and Eve learned after eating from the Tree of Knowledge, there is in life both good and evil. There is that which promotes life and there is that which does injury to it—or worse. But even the longest and happiest life is not, at least in this world, forever. The themes of evil and mortality, or evil and death, topics we would rather not have to confront, are most sharply brought before our attention by the issue with which our Parshah today begins, the issue of mortal human conflict.

Why, we ask, would an all-good, all-powerful and all-knowing God permit evil? Why, even if preceded by many years of health and happiness, is there death? Lest you think that the focus of my remarks will be on the negative, let me begin with two qualifications to the contrary. First, as Rabbi Pritzker has pointed out, our Torah, while recognizing the reality of death and evil, focuses on life itself. In protest against the Egyptian preoccupation with death and the afterlife, our Torah concentrates on the moral, experiential and spiritual enhancement of life.

My second point should, thus, be understood as complementary or supplemental to this original focus. I mention it only because so many today mistakenly believe that it is entirely absent in Judaism. What is it? If you can you hold your breath, I will get to it in a moment. But before that let me note that in the face of our perplexity at the negatives in human life Hebrew scripture values trust, trust in God, beyond a full intellectual comprehension as to why we undergo much that we undergo. Trust that there is a Source of meaning who governs life can provide us with a feeling of inner security, even in the face of suffering and adversity. This was the answer that Job received after undergoing severe loss and anguish. In the words of the Psalmist, "Yea, though I walk in the valley of the shadow of death, I shall not fear evil, for You are with me." That is, even if evil occurs, we may overcome feelings of absurdity and despair by virtue of our faith that we are not alone, that God governs the world and is with us.

I find it interesting that this approach is present in the Bible. For the Bible and later Jewish religious literature actually provide a more fully spelled out approach to the difficulties which evil and mortality present to our attempt to make sense of the world. It is as if our religious texts are saying, "Here is a fuller explanation which may instill in you a feeling of the infinite meaningfulness of life. But a fundamental trust that there is meaning is available to you simply through faith itself." It is that additional explanation which I now wish to explore, and to it I shall proceed immediately.

Judaism states that the world as it is and the life we now see are not all that there is or will be. For God did not simply create the world and leave it to function on its own. Rather God has a purpose in the creation of the world and that is that it should ultimately be a morally and spiritually perfected world. One day, Judaism says, there will not be war. There will not be hunger. There will not be the oppression of one person by another. One day the world will reach what we call redemption. The liberation of slaves from Egypt, our ancestors, was a foretaste of that ultimate redemption. But if this redeemed world, if this utopia, is one day achieved, then it would be unjust if it were enjoyed only by the generation which was the first to experience it, along with its successors. Renewed life will be experienced by all who went before.

I realize that this view may sound extraordinary to many in our time, but it is present in our tradition. I can only note, without going into it in this sermon, that even in the field of science the notion that the physical bodies of those alive at one time may be reconstituted or reformed in the future has already been discussed and argued for by a noted physicist, Frank Tipler, in his work, *The Physics of Immortality: Modern Cosmology, God and the Resurrection of the Dead*. But before discussing any further the concept of a perfected world in which such new life is achieved, I should first note that life eternal, according to our tradition, is not simply something which shall commence at that later date, in what we call the Messianic age. Immortality, in an unembodied form, in a plane beyond this one, is a reality already. This is that second point to which I referred above, which I said is believed by many in our time to be absent in Judaism, namely, the belief in life after death. Not all Jews today or in the past have believed it. The Sadducees, for example, opponents of the Pharisees, or early rabbis, did not believe it. But it is present in the Bible, in the prayerbook and in much other Jewish religious literature. That is not the case, however, because we believe that just existing or going on is a value in its own right. Rather a life of goodness is the truest way to taste life in its fullest. In this way, even if we suffer, we are not abandoned to feelings of meaninglessness or worthlessness. Still beyond the pleasures and adversities of this world there is, Judaism affirms, life at a higher, spiritual plane. Physical death is not the end of our existence.

In much of what is to come I will suggest how it may be possible for a person in our time to adopt this belief—or at least consider it. But, first, I will begin not by examining the mystery of death, but the mystery of — birth. A person, insofar as we are able to grasp the process, comes into being by her parents contributing the physical substance out of which she is formed and develops. And yet, the result of this process is something—or better, someone—who displays traits which are unexplainable through physical science. For one thing she manifests moral concerns, concerns about right and wrong, and cannot, in the depths of her being, be persuaded that these are just her personal, subjective, human feelings. Even the person who claims that that is the case protests against a wrong committed against him and does not feel that his anger against the wrong is just his subjective feeling. A person seeks to understand what is the spiritual meaning of this world in which he finds himself. A person, unless suffering from a clinical depression, has a feeling of inherent worth and dignity which would make no sense if he were nothing more than a meaningless clod of earth. All these traits are very strange and mysterious if the biological explanation of who we are were the whole story.

Let me make a comparison. Imagine that you were scrambling an egg and suddenly the egg began to say, "More gently, please. You're stirring too vigorously. You know, I have my dignity. You can't treat me any which-way you like." If an egg began to behave that way, wouldn't you begin to wonder if there were something more to the egg than the outer, physical substance of which it is made? That something more, when we speak of a human being, is usually called the soul. That is what feels and thinks and is concerned about matters of morality and spiritual meaning.

Now you may say, "But wait a minute. A person is really still just a body. For changing the body, through, for example, the introduction of coffee or alcohol or some other substance into it, will bring about a change in the person's consciousness, or what you call the soul. And when a person gets older, changes in the physical brain may bring about changes—serious changes—in the ability to think and reason. How can you say there is a soul? And if you go so far as to say that that soul can exist separately from the body, for example, in another plane, well, isn't that ridiculous?"

In answer, let me say that no one would suggest that the soul is unaffected by the body. But to be affected and even normally dependent on something is not to be identical with it. Perhaps people in this world are embodied souls. Perhaps the body is the vehicle through which the soul expresses itself. So, for example, when a person smiles at you, there is something more going on than her facial muscles getting arranged in a new way. Perhaps there is a soul trying to touch you. Perhaps in this life the relation between the body and soul is so close that each can affect the other, though they are not identical. We have noted how physical changes can affect your consciousness. But changes in your thought, that is, at the soul or mind level, can affect your body. If, for example, your mind believes there is danger, your heart may begin to pound and your skin may become covered with sweat. If you hear something happy, your eyes, your physical eyes, may light up. Though we are embodied in this world, at a different plane the soul, not identical with the body, can perhaps go on to live without it. What is considered believable changes from age to age. There was a time when this was considered a pretty unextraordinary thought. So long as the mystery of our birth exists, so long as we cannot explain how we got to be more than mindless physical objects, but beings with consciousness and conscience and a quest for meaning, the mystery of our death, the question of what happens to that more that we are, remains. Life beyond death remains a possibility.

I do not believe that there is any evidence which conclusively demonstrates the reality of life beyond death, but it is still helpful to listen to reports of those whose experiences may be able to teach us. I am referring, first, to the work of Dr. Raymond Moody, author of an influential book called *Life After Life*. Moody, at one point in his career, began to hear unusual accounts from patients who had had what are called near-death experiences, experiences of people at the point of death. He wrote up a summary of the characteristic features of these experiences, which I shall read to you now. Moody writes,

A man is dying and, as he reaches the point of greatest physical distress, he hears himself pronounced dead by his doctor. He begins to hear an uncomfortable noise, a loud ringing or buzzing, and at the same time feels himself moving very rapidly through a long tunnel. After this, he suddenly finds himself outside his own physical body, but still in the same immediate physical environment, and sees his own body from a distance, as though he is a spectator. He watches the resuscitation attempt from this vantage point and is in a state of emotional upheaval. After a while, he collects himself and becomes more accustomed to his odd condition. He notices that he still has a "body," but one of a very different nature and with very different powers from the physical body he has left behind. Soon other things begin to happen. Others come to meet him and help him. He glimpses the spirits of relatives and friends who have already died, and a loving, warm spirit of a kind he has never encountered before —a being of light—appears before him. This being asks him a question, nonverbally, to make him evaluate his life and helps him along by showing him a panoramic, instantaneous playback of the major events of his life. At some point, he finds himself approaching some sort of a barrier or border, apparently representing the limit between earthly life and the next life. Yet, he finds that he must go back to the earth, that the time for his death has not yet come. At this point he resists, for by now he is taken up with his experiences in the afterlife and does not want to return. He is overwhelmed by intense feelings of joy, love, and peace. Despite his attitude, though, he somehow reunites with his physical body and lives. Later he tries to tell others, but he has trouble doing so. In the first place, he can find no human words to describe these unearthly episodes. He also finds that others scoff, so he stops telling other people. Still, the experience affects his life profoundly, especially his views about death and its relationship to life.

Now, of course, you may say, "But still the brain of the person must have been functioning to at least a slight degree. Perhaps that remaining slight activity explains the unusual experiences these people had. After all, if there is life after death, why has no one appeared to confirm to us that there is?" To begin with, I should note that there have been near-death experiences in which no brain waves were present. Secondly, I should make mention of instances in which it at least seems that a person, from beyond this life, has, indeed, appeared. That is, there are alleged apparitions of those who are no longer in this life. I realize that this may all strike you as hooey. But I would remind you of the comment of that great American philosopher and psychologist, William James, after whom the psychology building at Harvard University is named, regarding the leading parapsychological journal of his day. As he writes, "Were I asked to point to a scientific journal where hard-headedness and never-sleeping suspicion of sources of error might be seen in their full bloom, I think I should fall back on the *Proceedings of the Society for Psychical Research.*" And the same moral-intellectual rigor is present, I would submit, in the most serious parapsychological investigators since James' time. One can, therefore, claim, if one wish, that a reported experience is subjective in origin. But one cannot simply claim that it could never have occurred. Beyond this, however, one can check whether the person seeing the apparition learned something which he could have found out in no normal way. If he did, then the appearance of a deceased person becomes a possibility and the notion that the experience is purely subjective in origin is thrown into doubt.

Let me give you an example. It took place during the Israeli War of Independence. A man is leading his platoon, walking in a single line through the dark night. Suddenly, he sees, as it were, a flame before him and beyond the flame, his deceased father motioning him to stop. He does and when the men examine the spot, they discover a mine which would have exploded, killing the platoon leader and perhaps one or more men behind him. Now you may say, "All right. Something unusual did occur here. But it wasn't the platoon leader's father appearing to him. Rather there is some form of extrasensory perception, whereby we can learn in a nonordinary way what is in our environment. When we do, we may imagine that someone from beyond is providing us with this information." I must admit that that is at least a logical possibility. But it is not certain. The straightforward explanation that the platoon leader was informed by his deceased father is also logically possible. I might mention that the platoon leader to whom I have referred was the father of our chazan, Cantor Aryeh Finklestein, and the man motioning toward the flame was the chazan's grandfather.

You may ask, "Why do some people have these experiences and others, not?" I cannot say. But let me make a comparison. What if the mind is like a radio and if it is in a certain state, or if you wish, set to a certain station, it picks up vibrations or information coming in. But we don't know how to pick up these vibrations at will, how to, so to speak, set our mental radio to the right station. If you should think it strange to speak of vibrations of which we are unaware, just think of the fact that this room, this very moment, is filled with vibrations of which we are unaware. If a radio were turned on here, we would suddenly become aware of all kinds of vibrations, producing music and other information, in which we might find great interest. Perhaps in our embodied state our mental radios are set to pick up information normally only from the physical plane. But even if it happens only rarely, what explains the information that we don't get through normal means?

At this point, I should recall that our tradition holds out the hope not only of life after death, but of a morally and spiritually perfected world in which both evil and death are overcome once and for all.

Is this all a fantasy? Is there a foundation to this hope? In today's sermon I have attempted to provide only a few suggestions as to why that for which we hope may, indeed, lie before us in our individual and common future. Perhaps one day war will be overcome and evil will cease. Perhaps as the prophet Isaiah says, the day will come when God "will swallow up death forever and... wipe the tear off of every face." But if we have doubts and questions, perhaps the counsel of our tradition to trust that there is meaning even when we don't understand is also available to us.

I will close today's sermon with these words taken from our weekday evening service. "Blessed is God by day. Blessed is God by night. Blessed is God when we lie down. Blessed is God when we rise up. In Your hands are the souls of the living and the dead, the life of every creature, the breath of all flesh. Into Your hand I entrust my spirit. You have redeemed me, O God, Divine Source of truth."

May the God of truth and of hope and of life be our solace and strength today and forevermore.

BEYOND THE CHAINS OF ILLUSION
A Sermon for Passover

I was about twelve years old at the time, and I was attending a friend's birthday party. That year, as every year, his parents hired a teenager to entertain us by performing magic tricks. When he reached one trick, I did something for which I claim no special aptitude. I had never done it before, and I have never done it since. As the trick progressed, the magician showed us an egg, or more precisely, a wooden replica of an egg, which was presumably going to end up in one place, while we thought it was in another place. When he finished the trick, he asked us where the egg was. I said, "in the bag." He was amazed. I was right.

How did I—on this one occasion—see through the machinations of a magician? It was simple. While he delivered his diversionary patter, I just watched his hand as he put the egg in the bag. He didn't even do it fast. His actions were out in the open, plain as day. Yet, we may say he was truly an illusionist, though not by making people see something which was not there. Rather he made people not see what was right before their eyes.

Today we begin our celebration of *Yetziat Mitzrayim*, or the Exodus from Egypt. Interestingly, the word *Mitzrayim*, or Egypt, is related to the word, *Metzarim*, which means straits or places of confinement and constriction. In the Hasidic tradition, the tales we read in the Torah are not simply events of the past, but have a present reality and urgency. Thus, the liberation in days of yore is one which we may also, God willing, experience today. It is one to which God is trying to draw us now. But we may, God forbid, choose to resist God's liberationist effort or simply make no effort to complement His. We may choose to remain within the *Metzarim*, the straits, which bar us from a full encounter with ourselves, our fellow human beings, the world and God Himself. The truth may lie before our eyes. But we may prefer our illusions, despite their consequences for us and for those we have loved and might still come to love.

I have decided to call today's sermon, "Beyond the Chains of Illusion," which is taken from the title of a book by the late psychoanalyst, Erich Fromm. Fromm recognized that the comfort, the security, the felt strength which limited perception and false belief give us are all ultimately illusory, and their price is great, perhaps even cutting us off from that which we might, in a clearer mind, view as priceless. Following Fromm's suggestion, I would say that Egypt is an ever-present danger. One may live in a democracy and still have difficulty seeing one's neighbor. One may attend a Seder and not be on speaking terms with the people at the Seder next door. Let us recall that each day we conclude the *Shema*, our most important prayer, with the words, *"Hashem Elokeichem Emet,"* "the Lord, your God, is truth." Judaism gives us great fulfillment, but it is not simply a feel-good religion. It is an effort to free us of illusions, so that we might meet God, life, each other and our own selves in truth and honesty.

If people are happiest when relations are good, how is it that relations sometimes get bollixed up? The following is surely not a complete explanation, but the problem arises, in part, from the fact that our perception of the other may be incomplete. I don't mean simply that we don't know everything there is to know about the other. To varying degrees, not always significant, that is, indeed, the case. But beyond that, there may be a very fundamental respect in which we do not adequately know the other. An easy example—that is, easy to intellectually grasp—is the problem which sometimes arises between members of different generations. I am thinking especially of the case where the parents may have grown up in a different cultural setting than the children. The same action may mean two different things, given the varying cultural backgrounds.

One case which comes to mind is that of a young woman I knew some years back who in early adulthood, not yet married, decided to live outside her parents' home. To us this might seem like a very innocent case. And yet, the parents, coming from a particularly strict Old World background, were horrified. Where they came from, only a loose woman would do such a thing. Let me note that the young woman in question was hardly a rebel. In fact, she was religiously committed, but in the way that you might expect in our country, that is, in the New World, and today, throughout much of the world. A young person, even committed to traditional ways, might, as she did, leave the family nest before finding a partner, without being immoral.

Now as I have said, the case just presented we would view as an innocent one. But how often do we ourselves believe that another person must come to a particular situation with the same perceptions we have? And if our values, as well as perceptions are right, and the person still acts in a way contrary to what we consider correct, then mustn't that person be possessed of bad motives and a bad character? Truly, from our standpoint, that person would be bad. But is it possible that there is a standpoint outside our standpoint? I don't mean that every time a person views things differently than us they are equally right. I am not a relativist. Not all judgments concerning a situation are equally valid. But to truly understand the other, must we not at least imaginatively attempt to stand within their standpoint, to experience things as they do? If not, how can we be certain that our perception is not simply an illusion, our judgment nothing but a false belief, no matter how intensely felt?

Now of course one would wish that all mistaken ideas about others were caused only by our not paying sufficient attention to the limits of our own understanding. The rabbis in the Talmud were too aware of human nature and behavior to be taken in that illusion. While not regarding us as innately sinful, the rabbis nonetheless paid serious attention to the *Yetzer Hara*, or evil inclination, with which every person must wrestle. Not all urges are for harmony. Not all urges are for respect. There is a pleasure which people may feel through a victory or sense of superiority over others. In the extreme case, one may wish to subjugate the other, and truly our ancestors tasted the bitter effects of this impulse during the time we call to mind today. Yet, as the philosopher Hegel noted, the master-slave relationship is one in which the top dog is living a shakier, more illusion-ridden existence than he realizes. For his sense of worth is dependent on the slave's acquiescence to his inferior position. When the slave rebels, the master suffers a psychological crash.

The rabbis, I must note, however, did not attribute problematic human relations only to the desire for power, and that may be the case even when a power-motive is present. There may also be the painful phenomenon which they termed *Sinat Chinam*, or enmity for the sake of enmity. When antisocial behavior is engaged in over and over, it may finally feel "good." Though negative in character, it may take on its own appeal. This phenomenon of *Sinat Chinam* the rabbis saw as the ultimate cause of the downfall of the Jewish commonwealth two-thousand years ago. Not the might of Rome, not the force of arms, but the denial of the worth and dignity of the other in *Sinat Chinam* was the ultimate cause.

What illusion was involved here? The illusion that actions have no consequences. The illusion that relations needlessly broken will not have an unforeseen impact, and then their restoration, fondly desired, cannot be counted on. In the case of direct interpersonal relations, the unforeseen impact may be the regret one feels oneself at the very absence of the relation. Now you may be surprised that I, who normally come across as a happy person, would be focusing, at least so far in this sermon, on the negative. I do not believe it is the whole story. I am not a pessimist. But neither am I pollyanish. The rabbis, who affirmed our creation in the image of God, the rabbis who affirmed that there is not only a *Yetzer Hara*, an evil inclination, but a *Yetzer Hatov*, a good inclination, the rabbis who affirmed the power of our free will to choose what this *Yetzer Hatov* is calling us to, still cautioned us to be aware of that which might lead away from such a choice. Forgetting that actions have consequences is one avoidable illusion which can hinder the realization of the *Yetzer Hatov* within us.

Let me tell you a story where the desire to have a positive effect, rather than all the details of the deed performed, itself brought about the desired consequence. Viktor Frankl, a world-renowned psychiatrist, was one night called by a man he had never met before. The stranger was in a suicidal state and wanted to meet with Frankl immediately. Otherwise, he was going to kill himself. Frankl went out and met him and they spoke for hours. Finally, the man said that he no longer wanted to kill himself. Frankl asked him what it was that he said which convinced the man. The man said it was nothing specific which Frankl had said. In fact, it turned out that the man did not even know that Frankl was a world-renowned psychiatrist. He had simply found his name in a phone book. To paraphrase the man's words from memory, he said, "You, a complete stranger to me, came out in the middle of the night to talk with me when I was in a desperate state. You have spoken to me for hours. I figure that if my life means so much to a complete stranger, then it should mean something to me." Here in Frankl we see what the rabbis call *Ahavat Chinam*, or love of another for its own sake. It's not that one likes the other. Frankl did not even know the man. It's not that one evaluates the other positively. Frankl did not even know what he looked like. But one affirms the other simply because this is the path of love, or in the language of our Mitzvot, because this is a realization of the commandment, *"V'ahavta l'reach kamocha,"* "You shall love your neighbor as yourself."

Not all instances of *Ahavat Chinam* need be so dramatic. I still remember—and can never forget—Dandy Sandy, the wonderful woman who used to be the cashier at the Coolidge Corner Bruegger's. When she brought you your coffee and rang up your order, she'd ask you, in the heartiest way, "How you doin', honey?" Her warmth, her friendliness, her cheerfulness, would give you a lift for a whole day. Or I call to mind Gayle Robinson, a guidance counselor at the Pierce Elementary School in Brookline, which Carol's and my daughter, Rina, used to attend. One day we were waiting in the auditorium for a program at the school to begin, and when Gayle came in and saw us, she gave us the most exuberant wave and "hello" across the room. It took all of a moment, yet its consequence is an enduring, warm, uplifting memory in our hearts.

Sometimes it seems as if we are living on two levels. We forget the deeper level within people where we may feel a kinship, notwithstanding differences. I am not suggesting that there are no cases where we may experience principled differences. But even then, I would suggest, there is a bond, a relationship, which also cries out for recognition. To make my point, let me take the most extreme case of conflict. Do you remember the Kursk, the Soviet submarine which became trapped beneath the waters? If it was not extricated, all of its sailors would die. If it was free and operative and there was, God forbid, war, this submarine, with its nuclear missiles, could have brought about the death of millions of Americans. And yet, our hearts went out to the endangered sailors. Tragically, the Soviet Union, fearful of us learning their secrets, refused American help, and all of the sailors died. And yet, we must not forget this strange—or rather beautiful—emergence into the light of day of a powerfully felt kinship between us and the sailors, simply as human beings to human beings. Am I suggesting that this is the only level of human relationship? I wish it were the case that I could say, "Yes," but I cannot. But neither is the real, yet more superficial level, where we more normally live. There conflict arises too easily or rather, I should say, when conflict

212

arises, we too often act as if it is the only level. When we realize it is not, we feel freed of an illusion. But as people suffering from an illusion are normally unaware that they are suffering from an illusion, they too seldom allow themselves to be directed by the wisdom of their higher selves.

God, speaking through the prophet Isaiah, tells us that the time will come when we will see not by the light of the sun or by the light of the moon, but rather by the light of God Himself. In that time we will see the divine spark in each person and find our fulfillment in the reinforcement of the bond which already implicitly exists between us. Today we celebrate our liberation from *Mitzrayim*, from Egypt. Let us also strive with all our might for a liberation from *Metzarim*, from the straits of self-confinement in which our illusions imprison us.

May the Lord cause His face to shine upon us now and—forevermore.

FEARFUL FREEDOM
A Sermon for Passover

As some of you know, I was in Detroit during the recent Chol HaMoed, or intermediary days of Pesach, visiting family. While there, I mentioned that I would be giving the sermon at Mishkan Tefila on this, the seventh day, of the holiday. My father asked me how long it was supposed to be. I told him that the people didn't want a talk that was really long. And so, in response he suggested to me an entire sermon which I might give. In fulfillment of the fifth of the Ten Commandments, which says, "Honor your father and your mother," I would now like to give you the sermon which my father recommended. Here goes.

"'Thou shalt be Jewish.'... Shabbat Shalom and Gut Yontif."

I know you enjoyed the brevity of this discourse, but perhaps something longer would be legitimate, if it could match this one in the richness of its content. And so, I shall now attempt a talk longer than "Thou shalt be Jewish"— but shorter than *Gone With the Wind*.

Water, water everywhere. Wherever we look in the Torah we find water and its conquest or its engulfing power or, on the other hand, its potential as a means of rescue or escape. Even as the latter, however, it is never to serve as a permanent residence, but only as a temporary abode until we reach dry land. When the Torah begins, we find the earth covered by water, as it is one massive ocean, with an island of land beneath. But God draws the water apart, revealing the hidden land, and it becomes the ultimate domain upon which we shall walk and live our lives.

When humanity as a whole, with only one exception, becomes sinful, God brings a flood to once again cover the earth, wiping out the wicked, so that there might be a new beginning with His moral-spiritual hero, Noah. When the Jewish people is imprisoned in the iron furnace of Egyptian slavery, Moses, the baby who is to become our leader in liberation, is placed in a basket on the Nile River, from whence he is discovered by the compassionate daughter of the Pharaoh. Water has served as a means of transporting baby Moses to a new site on dry land, where he might grow, free of the

Egyptian leader's genocidal designs, and ultimately become God's agent for our freedom. Ironically, as you know, this new site was in the Pharaoh's own palace.

Today, we have read of our people's final escape from the clutches of enslavement and tyranny, when the waters of the Red Sea split, enabling them to cross on and to dry land, while the pursuing Egyptians were drowned as the waters returned and covered them over. Interestingly, when Joshua, Moses' successor, later leads us into the Promised Land, the waters of the Jordan River stand erect, enabling the people to pass through. It seems that, in some important sense, dry land is our goal, or if not our goal, at least the place where we might seek to realize the goal around which our lives are organized.

Of course, this notion might be understood in the simple sense that we are creatures of the land, not fish, for whom water, rather than the open air, is the natural environment. The imperative to land on dry land is only biological and does not carry and deeper sense. Some might think that this is how we are to understand our first journey from, as it were, a watery realm to dry land, and by that I mean the trip we undergo from the wombs of our mothers to the world in which we dwell, a world no longer covered by the waters.

But, I think, a deeper significance lies within even this first journey, one dramatically highlighted in the story we read today, of the passage through, but more importantly, to dry land. For the dry land, with its open space and open air, symbolizes, I believe, the realm of freedom. We are not floating in outer space, but, at the same time, the very environment in which we dwell does not press in upon us. True, we do not have the security of the womb, but we do have the freedom to move and to act out our choices. Slavery, which took place in the realm of the dry land, was nonetheless not this sphere in its true and complete character. Perhaps we were not drowned, as were the people in Noah's time (though, of course, the Pharaoh did attempt this vis-a-vis the Jewish boys). But even if not drowning, the freedom symbolized by the open space, the open air, of dry land was not our lot. For this we had to cross the Red Sea and then begin the true journey in freedom.

The journey from the original watery realm, the womb, is a process by which we become a being possessing the mysterious power of free will, the ability to make decisions and take actions not simply based on instinct, not simply based on a program which nature or God might breed into us. As beings possessing this freedom, the freedom of free will, we can also not simply rely on past experience as a guide as to how to act in the future. For situations may rise which, however, similar to the past, are not identical to it, and the old formulae might not fit the needs of the new reality. I should mention that I am not suggesting that in this life of free will we should totally throw aside past experience or live without laws to direct our action. That would certainly be incompatible with both the spirit and content of the Torah. But two people, widely experienced and living lives of Torah observance, do not nonetheless live identical lives. Challenges arise for each which they must independently and with courage confront.

Strangely enough, slavery may serve as a psychological protection for those who are afraid of such freedom. It's not comfortable, but the boss or the enslaver, as long as he does not kill, makes all the important decisions for you. Over time his actions may lead you to feel incapable of making decisions for yourself and that very prospect may scare you. Indeed, even after crossing the Red Sea, the Jewish people were frightened of the challenges of freedom and complained against Moses that he had led them into the realm of freedom. A similar phenomenon is sometimes seen with abused women. Others may wonder why they do not leave their persecuting husbands. Apart from fear of possible physical consequences, the fact is that they have often become psychologically dependent upon their tormentors. Whatever positive feeling they may get about themselves they get from these distorted personalities. In this they are not to be criticized, but to be empathized with and hopefully helped.

Freedom, we should note, may, however, be frightful not only for those who are in extreme situations. Freedom may be fearful for the normal individual. Life, we know, is characterized by development. We do not come out fully formed. Our early experience is at home, but then we must develop to the point where we are ready to go off to school. Later changes within us bring about both an awakening of sexual consciousness and an awareness of our greater independence as individual selves. We want, but are nervous with, our newfound inner freedom. Finally, one day we leave home and venture out from the womb of the family, hopefully not to reject, but at the same time, to no longer dwell physically within it, with the psychological support which that affords. Even if one loves and has close relations with one's parents and siblings, the buds of the individual self are opening up, and the flower we are each to become needs the sun of the wider world in which to spread forth. Or to use an ornithological metaphor, to spread our wings we need the open spaces of the wider world.

And in each one of the stages I have alluded to above, following the old formula, the formula of the previous stage, will not work. We are not simply chucking our old identity, but it is growing richer, opening out in a way which we could not have foreseen or understood in advance. For in order to understand the consciousness of a later stage we must already be there. We can empathize with people who are further along in life's journey than we are, but it would be presumptuous to believe that we understand their experience in the way that they do.

In addition, while the stages of life which people undergo may have overall similarities, there is still the uniqueness of the situations faced by each person. From the outside people may be very alike. But once you sit down and hear each person's story, you suddenly realize that each person is, as our tradition says, an entire world. Furthermore, if there are common themes in most people's lives, still the variations must be faced and experienced and confronted and lived. A person is not a tale in a book. A person is a conscious, living experiencer of all the challenges of his or her life. Would you tell a woman experiencing the pains of labor that that's nothing new? The same newness of her experience is also so of every adolescent anxiously trying to find his or her way in the newfound world of more adult experience. The entrepreneur starting his or her business is facing this new experience. Even the most conventional life is a journey on a road not taken.

This truth, that human life, a life of free will, a life of freedom, means going forward in the face of uncertainty and insecurity, not denying anxiety, but not being crushed by it, is something that was epitomized in the life of the first Jew, Abraham, to whom God said, "Go forth from your land, from your homeland, from your father's house *to the land which I will show you.*" Abraham marched on despite the fact that his destination, and the journey there, were not clear. Such an attitude, I would suggest, involves trust, the confidence that we should go forward even if the way is not totally illuminated.

During the period when our people's greatest enemies were in power, a leading literary critic and political thinker, Walter Benjamin, decided to flee from his German home to freedom. Benjamin had faced many difficulties and when he reached one location, he was told that the border into the next country was closed. This was the straw that broke the camel's back, and that night Benjamin committed suicide. The following morning the border was opened up.

Religious faith involves the recognition that our knowledge is finite. There is only one, namely, God, whose knowledge is infinite, and within that knowledge may lie possibilities which our limited perception may not grasp. Consider the story of the Binding of Isaac. The challenge for Abraham, in being asked to sacrifice his son, was not only that this would be the most extreme and heartbreaking act in which any parent could engage. That would be enough. But in addition Abraham was, in effect, being asked to destroy the only means for the continuation of the spiritual project to which he had devoted his life, namely, the initiation and propagation of the Jewish people. What possible meaning could there be in this perplexing and confounding situation? Yet, Abraham went ahead, and God's hand checked his before the horrifying deed could be performed.

The great Bible scholar, E.A. Speiser, has said that from Abraham we learn that if we, the Jewish people, persevere even when all seems lost, then all will not be lost. It is not by accident that the national anthem of the Jewish state is called *HaTikvah*, or The Hope. In order to hope one cannot have complete knowledge. In order to trust one must be without complete understanding. For if we knew all, there would be no need to hope or to trust. Yet, we trust that in the Infinite Compassion who is the source of life there are reservoirs of energy for life, sustaining us and impelling us forward, despite difficulty and danger, despite tragedy and sorrow.

We should note, furthermore, that in our journey of freedom, a journey characterized, yes, by moments of fulfillment, but also by times of uncertainty, we need not be perfect in order to advance. How illuminating it is that when our ancestor Jacob reached the new higher identity of Israel, after wrestling with an angel, he was limping. In this new higher stage of development he could go forward even if he no longer had the smoothness of movement of Fred Astaire. If I might be allowed a slightly more irreverent comparison, Larry Bird was not the most graceful of basketball players, but he could score—and no less importantly, enable others to do so.

Not needing to be perfect, we are also not entirely on our own in going forward. We are intertwined with others more than we realize, and it is for that reason that we speak of only six degrees of separation. Frankly, at least among Jews, I believe there are far fewer. I do not say this to make light of people's feelings of aloneness. But if they reach out, if they attempt to touch others even more needy than themselves, they will find that they are part of a human web from which escape is only illusory.

Our Torah begins with a story of the waters covering the earth. But then God parts the waters, so that dry land may be disclosed, enabling a life of freedom. We might have expected the story to be brought to a happy ending, with the people He ultimately chooses living a life of fulfillment in their Promised Land. But when the story of the Torah ends the people have not even made it to the Promised Land. The Torah story is one of being on the way. The Torah story is one where we have not yet arrived, where we must still choose, with uncertainty and with trust and hope.

Exiles from the wombs of our mothers, we are on a journey of greater depth and greater meaning than one in which we have been fully programmed in advance. In this journey, as imperfect beings, intertwined with others, we are confronted with the challenge of individual freedom. In this journey each of us counts, for freedom for the group would be meaningless if the group were composed of mere robots.

The message of Judaism is that *you* count. Possessor of the spiritual dignity of freedom, go forward, even if less than perfect, even if muddling at times. Intertwined with others, you may be confident that your greatest gift to others will be the story of courageous and meaningful choice which is the tale of your own life.

Shabbat Shalom and Gut Yontif.

"FOR LOVE IS STRONGER THAN DEATH!"
A Yizkor Sermon

I was a boy of about eleven at the time, and I was driving with my older cousin, Saul Rose. Suddenly, Saul began to speak about my paternal grandfather, Dovid Tzvi Wolok. I was amazed. My Zeida Dovid Tzvi had been dead for many years, and here, out of the blue, Saul felt compelled to speak about him. I had never met my grandfather. In fact, my mother had never met him, as he had died before my parents even knew each other.

This story, of Dovid Tzvi being mentioned at the most unexpected times, has occurred many times during my life. Not too many years ago my father had to go to the hospital for a, thank God, not serious matter. The woman at the desk in the waiting room saw his name and asked my mother if she was related to David Wolok. She said that, yes, she was. He was her father-in-law, but unfortunately she had not had the good fortune of meeting him before his death. The woman described how, as a little girl, she would go into his shop and he would act in such a kind and friendly way toward her. Even as an elderly woman, she could not forget.

I trust that there are many people who cannot forget. My grandfather was one of those sharp businessmen who during the depression gave people with no means goods "on credit." And as I speak to you today, during this Yizkor service, I think of the line from Song of Songs, "*ki azah chamavet ahavah*," "for love is stronger than death," and realize how it does not refer only to our love for our departed. The memory of a loved one, even the imparted memory of a loved one, may be a source of strength for we, the living. I do not believe that I have ever received a visitation from the soul of my Zeida Dovid Tzvi, and yet during the most difficult moments of my life I have experienced him as a sustaining force. Knowing that this kind, loving, caring, generous man was my grandfather has lifted me up and borne me forth in my personal journey upon this earth. We remember, and the love of those we have loved, the love of those we still love, nourishes us and sustains us. Their love is stronger than death.

At times the love of those who are not here may even literally give life to those who remain behind. My cousin, David Kasmer, from Dzialoszyce, the same small town in Poland from which my mother comes, did not have her good fortune of leaving Europe in the years before World War II. He was taken to a concentration camp and there, like our other sisters and brothers in these terrible circumstances, was not only treated in a physically brutal manner, but told through word and deed that he was without any worth and value. Luckily not singled out for death, David, in the camps, thought back to his days as a little boy. When he would go off to school, his mother would look through the window until she could see him no more. While told by the Nazis that he was nothing, he knew that he had meant everything to this woman. This memory literally sustained him and kept him in life. His energy and dynamism to this day seem like a gift from heaven.

Did I say heaven? Do we Jews believe in heaven? Endless life for its own sake is not a value in Judaism. And yet, it would be false to say that traditional Judaism has not seen death as a transition, rather than as a conclusion. In matters of faith, I do not believe that we can speak with certainty. The same individual may experience a tension between conflicting thoughts. I myself partake of the view that even here on earth we cannot give an adequate description of ourselves. The process by which we come into existence, at least as it appears to our eyes, is physical. But then we don't act like simply physical beings. We ask what is the meaning of existence. We experience pangs of conscience. We even consider certain things of greater value than existence. My humble view is that there is something greater in us right now and this greater something does not cease with death. There is no absolute proof, but what might count as possible evidence should not be rejected out of hand.

Let me tell you about Abe Nemeth. Abe is a friend of my parents and a retired professor of mathematics. He has a fantastic sense of humor and a radiant smile to go with it. I can also say that Abe is a great davener. I still remember him leading a Maariv service at the Shiva for my maternal grandfather, Moishe Dovid Stolsky, a man whom I once felt compelled to talk about when asked by an acquaintance if anyone besides my parents and siblings and I had lived in our house when I was growing up. He hadn't, but his warmth, ebullience and love were so great that he could not go unmentioned when the topic of *mishpocheh* came up. We were honored that Abe would honor him, so feelingly chanting from his Siddur, which was printed in Braille. For Abe is blind.

In the midst of lively conversation, Abe once told us about an unusual experience his mother had while pregnant with him. One night in a dream a relative from England seemed to appear to her and state that he would shortly be leaving this world. Would she please name her child after him? Abe's mother thought that this was a mere dream, and when Abe was born, he was not named after the relative. Shortly thereafter, news arrived that the relative had died.

Now this story, and other similar stories, are not in themselves proof of life after death. But in this day and age, when the universe, when space and time themselves have, through Einstein, have been discovered to be different than we, with our common sense, think, perhaps there should be an open mind about a possibility for which we hope and which may be real. As I have said, I believe that there is something is us which partakes of a higher plane, but which goes beyond our understanding. Our essence eludes our comprehension. So, faith is not proof. But it is not foolish.

Still we should not think that eternity in Judaism refers only to a life beyond. During an Aliyah before the Torah we say, *"v'chayei olam natah b'tocheinu,"* "for eternal life He has planted in our midst." The suggestion is that right now, in the present, we may experience eternal life. What can this mean? Life which was unending, but did not partake of any eternal value, life which kept on going, but was devoid of higher meaning, would not satisfy our spiritual hunger. We want to feel that there is something of lasting value in our lives. And for this reason, we thank God for imparting to us the Torah, which enjoins us to a life of compassion and righteousness, sensitivity and caring, holiness and service. This is the eternal in life right now. This is why we say, *"etz chayim hi lamachazikim bah,"* "it is a tree of life to those who hold fast to it." We may today taste of the Tree of Life and experience that which is eternal in the present. Therefore, our tradition asserts not simply the immortality of the soul, but the immortal meaning of the human being. Whatever lies beyond, it is possible to live this meaning until the last moment of one's strength and capacities.

The story is told of Rabbi Israel Salanter, the founder of the

Musar, or Ethics, movement, that he died far from home. A simple, unlearned man who superstitiously believed that it was dangerous to be alone with a dead person was with him on his final night. He was asked what were the great rabbi's final words. The man said that Salanter tried to convince him to not be afraid. It wasn't really dangerous to be alone with a dead person. He would be alright. In his final, fleeting moment Salanter brought eternity into this world through his kindness to a simple man. This is Torah.

Now, I believe, we on many occasions encounter that which is eternal in meaning, but do not always realize it. We seem, at times, to live on two levels. People may get us upset, but then something happens to them, and we are filled with worry for their well-being. Sometimes it seems as if the whole human race is living on two levels. I am thinking, for example, of the recent case of the Kursk, the Russian submarine trapped beneath the water. Here were sailors who, in a time of crisis, may have been ordered to fire nuclear weapons at the United States. And yet, when they were in danger, in fatal danger, our hearts went out to them. Suddenly, they were just human beings, fellow human beings.

Now I am not suggesting that we should act as if everyone was nice, and we should dispense with means of self-defense. And I don't mean that below the surface, only nice sentiments reside. But somehow, in the whole mix, it seems as if there is a level where we are freed from the delusional dimension of our perception of ourselves and others. At certain moments it breaks through, and in moral, spiritual sanity we see fellow human beings.

Love is not blind, said the British philosopher, John McTaggart. Rather it is the lack of love which is blind. Think of the following case. Your spouse, hopefully after many years, has departed. During life you grew upset each day, as he or she accidentally, but inevitably, spilled coffee on the morning newspaper. Now you miss so badly those coffee-stained newspapers. Some may say that this is only because the coffee stains remind you of your loved one. I do not believe that that is so. In love you now see the endearing quality of the imperfection of a coffee-stained newspaper. You see the newspaper in the way that an artist does, with its own unique character, with the charm which not only shines through, but is enabled by the blemish. We all want straight teeth for our children. But a grin through buck teeth is not ugly. Our goal must be to increase during life the magnitude of our loving perception, to realize that ninety-nine percent of what we get worked up over is *bubkes*. Love is not blind. Love sees. The Torah says, "Love your fellow person." This is not pie in the sky. This is sanity and beauty.

The memory of moments of beauty are a gift from the lives of our loved ones which remains within and sustains. In Biblical Hebrew, the word, *zachor*, for memory, is related to the word, *sachar*, which means reward. We are eternally rewarded by the imprint of our loved ones within us, which is memory. And their lives continue to work their effect within us with a force and reality which is unending.

The great American philosopher, Alfred North Whitehead, teacher of our beloved rabbi, Israel Kazis, of blessed memory, concluded his magnum opus, *Process and Reality*, with the following words:

"... the insistent craving is justified—the insistent craving that zest for existence be refreshed by the ever-present, unfading importance of our immediate actions, which perish and yet live evermore."

Let us cherish the memory of our departed loved ones, whose love for us is an eternal presence and undying blessing.

Part IV

FROM "WHY?" TO "HERE I AM":
MEDITATIONS FOR EVERY MOMENT

WHY?

What do I live for? What should I live for? Is there anything for which I must live, not for my own sake, so that I might feel fulfilled and uplifted, but for its sake, so that it might be served and realized? Is there anything which is truly ultimate, not because nothing greater can be found, but because nothing greater can be? Is there anything which obligates me absolutely, yes, fulfilling my self, but only because through it I am able to transcend myself?

As I seek after this anything, might I ask if it cannot be an anything, but rather only an anyone? For if I am a conscious being, if I am a person, how can the source of my heart's direction be a principle unaware of its own existence, no matter how lofty? If I am possessed of free will, how can the source of my soul's command be an ideal which is itself incapable of moral action and commitment? As I am an anyone, must I not receive my obligations from One who is not less than me? Rather than a concept which is the embodiment of goodness, must not the highest be an Anyone who embodies goodness and commands the good as an expression of His very being?

Service to others is not distinct from service to the One who is ultimate. He calls us to respond to the other. He calls us to attend to him, to love him, to raise up his spirits, to uplift his soul. He calls us to recognize the privilege of being of service to others, to appreciate the opportunity of enabling a light from above to make its way into our world of the everyday.

God, who dwells both on high and within the soul, bring me back to myself. Free me from the prison I am in when I hide within myself. To the *neshamah*, the soul, You have placed within me, impart Your *neshimah*, Your breath, so that I may be released, borne aloft, as I walk upon Your earth, encountering the face of stranger and friend, meeting the countenance of all my human kin.

Ana avda d'Kudsha Brich Hu.

For I am a servant of the Holy One Blessed Be He.

Va'ani tefilati l'cha.

May I be a prayer unto You.

A RITUAL DIRECTOR'S *HINENI*

At the beginning of the High Holiday Musaf service the cantor chants a prayer which is unique in the year's liturgy. It is called the *Hineni*, which means, "Here I am," and in it he expresses his concerns and hopes over his role, calling upon God to help him as emissary of the congregation.

The following is a ritual director's *Hineni*, which I have composed after seven years of service with the members of Mishkan Tefila.

O God, I thank You for the miracle of encounter, for the moment of meeting those into whose path I come.

Teach me to appreciate the importance of simply being there, of being present to those who are seized with grief and whose pain may be felt to be unbearable.

Teach me to support those at an earlier stage who, excited yet nervous, stand upon the threshold of adulthood within our community.

Teach me to value words, written and spoken, to young and old alike. For more than wanting things do they desire words of kindness and understanding. "You matter" means more than objects of matter.

Teach me to value teaching, whether the content taught be a skill or an idea for the mind—and the heart.

Teach me to sense that the heart desires song. Let our Torah be chanted. The meaning of the text and its music are one.

Teach me to value the experience of sharing in the happiness of others. Let me feel the beauty and dearness of tears of joy.

Teach me to be there and to give to those whom I meet in the "space" You have created called life.

God, let me know that I am a moment in Your eternal drama.

Let eternity fill it, so that time alone does not become the measure of my life.

Let me touch and be touched by my fellows, whom You have created.

And let this moment before You be—Amen.

Part V

IMAGINING THE EARTH:
A FANTASY

We were sitting at the Central Cafe on Main Street, having brunch one Sunday morning, when my friend suddenly asked, "Davin, do you know what this existence of ours is?" I said, "What?," and he answered, "We're on television programs being seen by beings on a higher plane." I responded "So how did we get on these programs?," and he shot back, "We got the best ratings!"

Now the notion that there is a higher plane of reality is not really foreign to Jewish thought. Contrary to what many today think, there is, for example, a belief in a world beyond ours, a world of eternal life. In fact, as one with an interest in music, I am enchanted by the mystical text which speaks of souls on high as singing during the night to God. Imagine that. Souls gather to *daven* to the Almighty, while we here on earth have to work to gather a Minyan. How come?

To be frank, I must admit that there is a consistency in the traditional thinking which portrays the worship "up there" as more easily achieved than the worship "down here." For the world-on-high is also regarded as a realm embodying perfection. What one finds there serves as a model for our existence here. We, not it, are in need of basic guidance. We, not it, need to *ascend*.

This thought came to mind when I was recently informed of a fascinating tale, "Imagining the Earth," whose authorship is anonymous and whose place of publication remains shrouded in mystery. It deals with a group of philosophers who have departed for the next world and who, when there, suffer sudden amnesia regarding their earlier existence.

Occasionally, one of the philosophers claims to recall a world very different from the one they currently find themselves in. It is a world of opposites, where people are constantly coming up with new gadgets and high-tech means of communication, but still have trouble understanding each other. Regarding themselves as more than animals, they nevertheless hesitate to go to houses of worship where spirituality might be cultivated. They care for friends in grief, yet fail to support religious services at which mourners might recall their loved ones who have gone. This world is a contradictory and confusing one.

The other philosophers, of course, do not believe that the "recollections" are of anything real. How can there be a place with so many inconsistencies? Surely people would feel thankful for their plentiful blessings and wish to express themselves in prayers of gratitude. Surely sensitivity to others in grief would translate into attendance at services in support of mourners. And surely those observing the anniversary of the death of a loved one would be backed by a community in which thoughtfulness is present and consideration is not an unheard of phenomenon. Experts at the techniques of communication, the people of this confusing world must surely empathize with those who need their empathy. No. This world "recalled" by a few amnesiac philosophers must be a fantasy. "It's all in their mind," the majority say. Rest and relaxation will cure them of their delusion.

One day a philosopher of a religious orientation suggests a new approach to the question of the "lower world." He claims that there can be no certainty regarding the existence of this world, normally called "earth." Still there is a value in making a "leap of faith" that it exists. "Things don't have to be perfect to exist," he says. "And if less-than-perfect things exist, they can strive for perfection. Then we, too, may have a purpose, to serve as their model. We will be the inspiration for the people on earth."

Notwithstanding the skepticism of the other philosophers, the religious conception begins to win the day. In addition, a more emotional conception of philosophy begins to establish itself. No longer will philosophy be an exploration of the intellect alone. Rather allied means of stirring an awareness of the divine will be drawn upon and utilized. Foremost among them will be music. For if as one thinker said, "Philosophy is the music of the soul," so, too, is it the case that, "Music is the philosophy of the soul." Song, not thought alone, will awaken in earthly souls an awareness of the spiritual. Thus began the singing to God at night. And thus began the hope-on-high that their *davening* would inspire our own efforts at prayer.

Finally, after the passage of much time the day comes when the amnesia of the philosophers begins to wear off. It is said that some, in regaining their memory, became depressed at the inconsistencies of earthly existence. Others became more convinced than ever of the critical role they played in our struggle for a higher way of life. The story leaves off before all the philosophers have fully regained their memory.

However fantastic this tale by author unknown, however suspicious the mystery of its creation, we may still reflect on what it suggests about our efforts "here below." In a word, it is that our deeds matter. We may not see anything of eternal meaning in what we do, but that meaning is still there. In the modest locale of a chapel, in the humble modality of a Minyan, we may engage in something of transcendent worth. When our prayer rises up and we give support to those who grieve and who remember, we should realize that our efforts are sought by a plane we may not see, but which calls out to us—and needs us. When we care for others and show up on their behalf, we are performing a Mitzvah of ultimate significance.

So, then, do we get the best ratings? The answer is up to us.

Breinigsville, PA USA
26 March 2010
235000BV00001B/1/P